AF564707

SELF EVALUATION IN STUDENT TEACHING

SELF EVALUATION IN STUDENT TEACHING

Digumarti Bhaskara Rao
M.Sc., M.A., M.A., M.Ed., Ph.D.

Chilukoti Anantha Padmanabha Swamy
B.Sc., M.Ed.

Bulusu Surya Venkata Dutt
M.A., M.Ed.

R.V.R. COLLEGE OF EDUCATION
GUNTUR—522 006
ANDHRA PARADESH

DISCOVERY PUBLISHING HOUSE
NEW DELHI—110 002

First Published - 1997

Reprinted - 2016

ISBN: 978-81-7141-374-4

Self Evaluation in Student Teaching

Published by:

DISCOVERY PUBLISHING HOUSE PVT. LTD.

4383/4B, Ansari Road, Darya Ganj

New Delhi-110 002 (India)

Phone: +91-11-23279245, 43596064-65

Fax: +91-11-23253475

E-mail: discoverypublishinghouse@gmail.com

sales@discoverypublishinggroup.com

web: www.discoverypublishinggroup.com

Printed at:

Infinity Imaging Systems

Delhi

CONTENTS

CONTENTS (Contd.)

PREFACE

The strength of any educational system largely depends upon the quality of its teachers. However enlighted the aims, however up-to-date the equipment, however efficient the management, the education of children is determined by the teachers. Therefore, there is no important matter than that of securing a sufficient supply of the right kind of people to the profession, providing them with the best possible training and ensuring to them a status and esteem commensurate with the importance and responsibility of their works. And with the rapid expansion of schooling, both in numbers and extent, the teachers must come out of teacher education institutions with great perfection in teaching and allied aspects.

The success of the teachers much depends on their knowledge of set of methods, their possession of quantity and quality of content, their interests and habits, their imaginativeness and sympathies, the balance and poise of their character, their knowledge of children and environment, and their self-evaluation of their own teachings.

The consideration given to the self-evaluation of lessons in student teaching and in-service teaching puts these researchers on track to make the prospective teachers evaluate their lessons during their student teaching period. By self-evaluation of their lessons, the prospective teachers have expressed much satisfaction about their teaching. They have got satisfaction with their use of teaching strategies, educational technologies, teaching procedures, classroom management, etc. They have also felt that they can improve their teaching by additional teaching.

The book, we hope, will help the teacher educators and prospective teachers in developing effective teaching strategies and the researchers in conducting experiments to improve the quality of teacher education.

CARE Educational Consultancy
4/18, Barodipet
Guntur — 522 006

D. B. Rao
C.A.P. Swamy
B.S.V. Dutt

Acknowledgements

We are thankful to Dr. Sunil Behari Mohanty, A.A. Training College, Fakirpur; Mr. M. Nageswara Rao, J.K.C. College, Guntur, Mr. P.Koleswara Rao, Vignan Degree College, Vadlamudi; Dr. L. Ratvaiah, Vignan Educational Institutions, Guntur, Vizag. and Hyderabad; Mr. V. Venkateswara Rao, Ravindra Bharathi Public School, Vijayawada; Mr. Ganta Nageswara Rao, Noble Educational Academy, Guntur; Dr. K.R.S. Sambasiva Rao, Nagarjuna University, Nagarjunanagar; Mr. N.S.R. Prasad, Junion College, Inkonu; Mr. G. Sundara Rao, A.L. College of Education, Guntur; Mr. R. Ranga Rao, A.J. College of Education, Guntur; Ms. B. Veena Kumari, Sir C.R.R. College of Education, Eluru; Mr. Y. Jaya Sankara Prasad, G.H.R. & M.C.M.R. College, Guntur; Mr. B. Venkateswara Rao, Andhra Muslim College, Guntur; Mr. Srinivasa Babu, Andhra Muslim College, Guntur; Dr. K. Subba Rao, Andhra University, Waltair; Dr. B. Manmohan Singh, Osmania University, Hyderabad; Dr. U.L. Narayana, Regional Institute of Education, Mysore; Dr. Padmanabhaiah, S.V. University, Tirupati; Dr. G. Ramesh, Kakatiya University, Warangal; Mr. G.M. Madhukar, A.L. College of Education, Guntur; Mr. P. Narasimha Rao, CARE, Guntur; Dr. Dutt, A.N.R. College, Gudivada; Mr. L. Papa Rao, Vignan Cooperative College, Guntur and Mr. Ravindra Babu, Subhasya Chit Funds and Finance Private Limited, Guntur for their manual, material and moral help.

We are also thankful to the Principals, Staff and Students of Rayapati Venkata Ranga Rao College of Education, Guntur and Andhra Luthern College of Education, Guntur.

Sai Soudha
D–43, S.V.N. Colony
Guntur–522 006

Dr. D. Bhaskara Rao
C.A. Padmanabha Swamy
B.S.V. Dutt

1

INTRODUCTION

Any system of education does not rise higher than the level of its teachers. The quality of education is also largely determined by the effectiveness of the practicing teachers. The teachers decide the fate of the pupils and progress of the nations. They can also make the education a thing of joy and success and or a matter of frustration and failure. Now-a-days the teacher's role is changing as he is an important man in the society. He has to serve the community besides helping his students learn the prescribed subjects and handling the sophisticated educational technologies. Hence, selection and training of teachers are the important aspects of teacher education.

INTRODUCTION TO STUDENT TEACHING

Pre-service and in-service education are the two major areas of teacher education. Pre-service teacher education is concerned with the training of would-be teachers and in-service teacher education is concerned with the provision of orientation and refresher programmes which keep the teachers upto the expected levels in the changing society with the changing needs of the students. But, pre-service teacher education is very crucial component of teacher education as it prepares the future teachers.

Pre-service teacher education has two aspects—theoretical studies and practical activities. The theoretical components help the would-be teachers equip themselves with the knowledge of various dimensions of teacher education and the practical components help them acquire the essential teaching skills.

Practicals in teacher education are generally of three categories-practicals on theory subjects, practicals on work experience and community development, and practicals on school work. The last category of practical work is known as student teaching, practice teaching, internship etc. The practical work play a vital role in deciding the teacher effectiveness.

Objectives of Student Teaching

Objectives of student teaching help in explaining the details of various teacher education programmes. All institutions should have written objectives for student teaching.

The following objectives of student teaching were suggested by Mohanty.

1. To provide an opportunity for applying theory in practical situations.
2. To possess maximum technical know-how and skills in preparing and use of instructional materials including teaching aids.
3. To use available human and material resources effectively.
4. To assume gradually and finally the responsibility of a teacher.
5. To practice skills and develop competence in relating learning materials, the techniques of teaching and instructional materials to the needs of the school students and to the needs of the community.
6. To develop professional attitudes.
7. To be aware of different evaluation devices and tools and their application in knowing the growth of the student.
8. To be aware of and to perform non-classroom teaching duties of a teacher.
9. To develop satisfactory relationship with students.
10. To identify exceptional learners and to assist them.
11. To budget the syllabus according to the amount of time and resources available.

12. To understand the process of curriculum development and to develop skills in planning various types of lessons using varieties of methods and strategies.

Bhaskara Rao prescribed the following objectives for student teaching.

1. To equip the student teacher thorough with knowledge of content.
2. To make the student teacher aware of various teaching strategies.
3. To give opportunities to student teachers to put their abilities and skills into practice.
4. To avail the student teachers use of audio visual teaching aids.
5. To develop professional attitude in student teachers.
6. To observe the student teachers the problems and prospects associated with teaching profession.
7. To develop an interaction with schools and their various components.
8. To understand the role of teachers in school and community.
9. To make the student teachers competent teachers.

But the objectives of student teaching vary from course to course and place to place depending various factors.

Preparation for Student Teaching

Preparation for practice teaching plays are important role in the student teaching programme. Before student teachers go to schools to participate in practice teaching activities, they should be prepared for it. The areas of preparation for student teaching are: enrichment of content knowledge, observation of classroom teaching of good teachers, preparation and use of audiovisual aids, knowledge of preparation, administration and scoring of standardized tests, administration and scoring of standardized tests, preparation of case studies of children, maintenance of cumulative records, maintenance of health cards use of first aid, maintenance of records used in schools, planning of individual lessons, planning of units of teaching preparation of a scheme of work, maintenance of teacher's diary, participation in physical education, organization of field trips, organization of quest talks, organization of exhibitions, organization and participation in parent teachers associations, visits to homes of school students, organization of project work, giving assignments, organization of club activities, community development work by school, organization of functions and festivals in school, organization of debates, seminars, symposia, elocution, contests, song competitions, etc., review of school curriculum, mastering of a number of skills, teaching in a small group of peers (simulated teaching), teaching in a small group of school students, and teaching in a normal class.

In order that the student teachers develop properly in teaching the teacher educators deliver or arrange demonstration lessons. These lessons are the models to student teachers covering different types of contents and teaching strategies. Once demonstration lessons are given, the teacher education institutions go ahead with the development of teaching skills in student teachers. When teaching preparation comes to a desired level, the student teachers are sent for practice teaching (Mohanty)

The planning necessary for student teaching is as follows.

Before admission of student teachers

1. Organization of staff meeting at the teacher education institution level to decide

   a. Method masters for different subjects

   b. Method master and student teachers maximum ratio

   c. Co-operating school for practice teaching

   d. Schools to be visited by student teachers

   e. Teachers whose class room teachings are to be observed by student teachers

   f. Minimum number of days for which a student teacher should attend a school for student teaching programmes

   g. Staff members act as lessen officers for co-operating schools.

   h. Nature of the training programme for student teachers;

   i. Nature of the training programme for co-operating teachers

j. Programmes for

i) Demonstration lessons

ii) School visits

iii) Screening of educational aids

iv) Training in different audio visual teaching aids, preparation and their use

v) Criticism/discussion of lessons

vi) Guest talks.

vii) Method theory classes

viii) Training in different teaching skills

ix) Training in community development and other skills

x) Training of co-operating teachers

k) Details of

i) Schools observation sheet

ii) Classroom teaching observation sheet

iii) Profile plan for student teachers for use of method masters

iv) Proforma for assessment of classroom teaching performance of student teachers

v) Proforma for assessment of other activities of student teachers

vi) Proforma for supervision of student teaching, classroom teaching and other activities of student teachers

vii) Proforma for recording bio-data of student teachers

viii) Proformas for bio-data sheet for school teachers and staff members of teacher education institutions

ix) Guidelines for student teachers and co-operating

school-heads and subject teachers

x) Information sheet on schools for selection of schools for visit and practice teaching

xi) content knowledge test for student teachers

l) Making provisions in the time table for

i) School visits

ii) Audio-visual education training

iii) Training in skills of teaching

iv) Demonstration and criticism/discussion of lessons

v) Feedback seminars on student teaching

vi) Lesson plan correction

vii) School visit by staff members of teacher education institution

2. Collecting data about schools and teachers working in the schools for practice teaching and visits by student teachers.

3. Supplying co-operating schools with bio-data of staff members, relevant books, journals, teaching aids available for school use, a copy of the syllabus, etc.

After Admission of student teachers

4. Orienting students teachers about the teacher education institution and providing a bird's eye view of the students teaching programme..

5. Conducting a content knowledge test of student teachers in case of those who have not studied a method subject at their graduation stage.

6. Showing various educational films to student teachers.

7. Providing training to student teachers on

a) Preparation and use of audio-visual aids

b) Skill in teaching through

i) Micro-teaching

ii) Interaction analysis

iii) Transaction analysis

iv) Role play and simulation

c) Teaching Techniques for self study and group study

d) Individual and team teaching techniques

e) Preparation of work sheets and programmed learning materials.

f) Organization of

i) Exhibitions

ii) Field strips

iii) Functions, festivals and dramas

iv) Guest talks

v) Parent Teachers Association

vi) Project work

vii) Seminars and debates

ix) Outdoor lessons

x) School complex

g) Correction of home work.

h) Techniques of observation of schools

i) Preparation, administration, scoring and interpretation of tests

j) Assessment of school curricula including text books, syllabus, etc.

k) Home visits

l) Action Research

m) First Aid

n) Adult literacy work

o) Case study of school children

p) Education of dropouts and left-outs

q) Office work

r) Community development work and utilization of community resources for school use and vice versa

s) Cumulative record card

t) Physical education

u) Health card

v) Physical Education

8. Organization of talks by different types of officials of administrative departments regarding their roles that have relevance to a teacher.
9. Organization of visits by student teachers to ideal educational institutions.
10. Training of student teachers in preparation of various types of lesson plans and schemes of lesson.
11. Organization of demonstration lessons covering varieties of techniques.
12. Organization of criticism/discussion of lessons.
13. Organization of orientation meeting of student teachers, co-operating teachers and staff members of teacher education institutions, before the student teachers are sent for practice teaching.

Resources for Student Teaching

Human resources and material resources are the resources for student teaching. Availability of these resources that are explained below determine the quality of the student teaching programme (Mohanty).

Human Resources Consist of the Following

1. Competent method masters who have studied the content at least in their graduation stage, have studied the said method at their M.Ed. or M.A. (Education) stages, and have been teaching at schools.
2. Audio-visual instructor
3. Laboratory assistant

4. Librarian
5. Research assistant
6. Physical education instructor
7. Health instructor

Material Resources include

1. Demonstration/laboratory schools which provide opportunities to student teachers to observe and participate in their activities, provide opportunities for college teachers to undertake classroom teaching and research and provide class for demonstration, criticism and practice teaching lessons and for evaluation of classroom teaching performances.
2. Co-operating schools of good quality in the vicinity of the college
3. Method subject-wise rooms in the college
4. Library with open access system
5. Reading room with relevant educational journals
6. Rooms for holding tutorials/discussions/seminars
7. Auditorium
8. Laboratory
9. Play-ground
10. Audio-visual room with facilities for storing various audio-visual aids including equipments.
11. Audio-visual equipments consisting of television, closed circuit television, video recorder, film strip projector, slide projector, overhead projector, epidiascope, tape recorder, cassette-recorder, record player, linguaphone, films, videotapes, audio cassettes, films, filmstrips, slides, transparency sheets.
12. Various types of proformas, observation sheets, etc., to be used in student teaching programmes are
    a) School observation sheet for student teachers
    b) Classroom teaching observation sheet for
        i) Peers
        ii) School teachers

iii) College method masters

c) Non-classroom teaching activities observation sheet for

i) School heads or co-operating teachers

ii) College method masters

iii) Peers

d) Feedback sheets for use of school students

e) School data sheets filled-up by school for use of college

f) Self-evaluation sheets for use of student teachers

g) Student-teacher bio-data sheet for use of schools

h) College staff member bio-data sheet for use of schools

i) Evaluation proforma

j) Blank profile for recording and evaluation of activities of a student teacher.

k) Guidelines for student teaching programme including roles to be played by various categories of personnel involved in it.

All the stated human and material resources may not be available in all teacher education institutions. The student teachers have to make use of the available ones to the best.

Assessment of Student Teaching

Assessment of student Teaching is a problematic subject (Stones). It consists of assessment of classroom teaching performance, ability to write a scheme of lessons, performance in non-classroom teaching activities, and writing of lesson plans. Classroom teaching performance is judged by observing one to five lessons, but the assessment of number of lessons varies from teacher education institution to institution.

The following aspects (Mohanty) may be considered for assessment of student teaching

1) Development of a proformas of assessment and evaluation of classroom teaching performance and related activities of student teachers.

2. Explaining the criteria of assessment to student teachers.
3. Assessing student teachers systematically and continuously.
4. Restricting the scale of assessment to a five-point scale.
5. The aspects to be valuated and weightages to various aspects of evaluation maybe as follows
   i) Classrooms teaching performance....50%
   ii) Maintenance of lesson plan....10%
   iii) Preparation of a scheme of lesson.....20%
   iv) Involvement in school programmes and activities besides classroom teaching....20%

Expertise is necessary to assess, evaluate and guide the student teachers. For this adequate training is necessary to supervisory personnel.

Supervision and Guidance in Student Teaching

In any student teaching programmes, supervision is an essential component. The supervisor of student teaching- may be a staff member of a teacher education institution or a school - is supposed to give guidance to the student teacher at the time of and after student teaching. For this effective student teaching supervisors are required. The co-students also aid the student teacher in providing feedback. Now-a-days, video cassette recorders and audio-cassette recorders are in use to get an effective feedback and to have a perfect guidance.

Anywhere in the world, there is no uniform pattern of supervision, feedback and guidance as it varies from institution to institution and from university to university. Because of this, there is a problem of standards and quality in teacher education. There is a problem of availability of trained and effective supervisors in order to supervise properly and guide the student teachers to the expected levels. There is a problem of proper proforma of evaluation. Also many teacher education institutions are not in a position to provide the latest recording facilities. The above problems deserve due attention.

Effective supervision, proper feedback and efficient guidance help the student teachers become good teachers in future.

Innovations in Student Teaching

Innovations refer to specific and planned changes within any process of reform (Thomas). Innovation alters, introduces something new or introduces novelties and changes. It accelerates the process of improvement of programmes. The accelerating and multiplying effect of new techniques of reproduction and communication is basic to the reproduction of most educational innovations (Learning to Be).

Innovations in student teaching programmes are very much useful as they inculcate creativity and bring out inner potentialities of the student teachers. Innovations in student teaching help student teachers develops proper attitudes, abilities, aptitudes and performances. Micro-teaching, performance-based or Competency-based teaching, Team teaching, etc., can be used in student teaching to develop the required teaching skills. This type of programmes according to the American Association of colleges for Teacher Education have the characteristics such as individualization and personalization of instruction, modularisation of instruction, shifting of emphasis on conditions from those of entry requirements, accountability of student teacher for one's performance, more systematization of programmes, and provision of feedback for learning. These programmes have not been immune to criticisms. The validity of competencies expected in these programmes have been questioned. There is also lack of unanimity among teacher training institutions about what the student teachers ought to achieve and the methods in which such achievements are to be made (Mohanty).

According to Rogers the stages of adoption of innovations are awareness, interest, evaluation, trail, and adoption. The person or institution first becomes aware of innovation already existing or newly to be introduced. Interest in the said innovation leads to evaluation of innovation in terms of objectives of a programme and on finding it useful, it may be tried out in the concerned programme and if found suitable may be adopted, for mass and permanent use.

Holmes has suggested nine stages for implementing an innovation. Those 9 stages are evaluating on-going programme, determining objectives to be changed and achievements to be improved, reviewing literature and studies pertaining to the said innovation, deciding method of implementation, deciding operational plans including summative and formative evaluation procedures, ensuring consensus and complete understanding of the plan by all concerned, providing necessary material and moral and organizational and administrative support, providing incentives for motivation and in-service training, and ensuring advertently change of social structure or organization.

Successful implementation and diffusion of innovations require planned organizational change (Hoyle). Hence any innovation without planned organizational change soon loses its ground. Implementation of innovation "require a lot of hard work and sharp awareness of the wide range of tasks and details that need to be attended over an extended period of time (Karmos and Jacko). They require sustained effort. They also require willingness of various personnel concerned in the process of implementation. They mostly appear because of voluntary actions. They get invented, planned, initiated, and implemented because of the initiatives of individuals or groups to make educational practice geared to changing objectives and standards (Hussen). It makes time for organizations and persons therein to be aware of innovations and their relevance to the improvement of programmes. Once a person is aware of an innovation, it becomes his or her responsibility to make the colleagues realize the usefulness of such an innovation, and evolve an consensus about its experimentation. Thus each innovation takes much time for implementation. It cannot be introduced hurriedly. Again, in the process of developing awareness, the person who initiates innovations should be a very good communicator. Ineffective communication is a serious impediment to change. Only trying out innovations is not adequate. The innovations should be institutionalized. This is the goal of each attempt for innovation. When an innovation is successful, it is to be institutionalized and practiced (Mohanty).

While participating in student teaching, the student teachers apply certain methods of instruction unnoticingly which deserve due attention by supervisors (Bhaskara Rao). Innovations come out of thinking, planning and practicing, and of course, sometimes by chance.

STATEMENT OF THE STUDY

A study of the role of self evaluation of lessons by the prospective teachers in enhancing their teaching efficiency.

NEED OF THE STUDY

Today assigning College or University credit to student teaching is a well-established practice. In the recent past, however, this issue was a battle ground for university educators and liberal arts professors. There is still little agreement among training institutions about the appropriate amount of course credit to be assigned to student teaching. The standards set by individual universities have resulted in a greater consistency among states in the assignment of credit for student teaching.

As the demand for more and better student teaching for more candidates has grown, training institutions have looked to the universities for support, if not leadership. In many parts of the country, department officials, school personnel and university educators have formulated comprehensive plans for both the regulation and the support of student teaching. While this is an encouraging development, there are no guarantees that there will be substantive improvements in the quality of student teaching. All, too frequently, the changes in student patterns are dictated by expediency and hunch rather than by comprehensive analysis of the training needs of the beginning teacher.

There is no component of teacher education which enjoys more support from the education community and which is evaluated so positively by beginning teachers as student teaching. As James B. Conant aptly put it, "Academic professors and professors of education are in complete agreement only on one point, that practice teaching, if well conducted, is important." However, while student teaching enjoys a very favourable reputation and is deeply entrenched, it is not without serious problems. A growing number of individuals inside and outside the profession are raising questions about the very nature of student teaching. To evaluate the strengths and weaknesses of student teaching, one must know the goals of the student-teaching programme and how they are implemented. Because of the very nature of student teaching, we lack data on both counts. L.O. Andrews of Ohio State University, an authority on student teaching, has synthesized the stated goals of many programmes. They are (1) to provide for a concentrated period of growth in professional and personal attributes, understandings, and skills of the teacher, and (2) to assist a student to discover if teaching is what he really wants to do and actually can do.

Student teaching's wide support in the teacher education community and its popularity with beginning teachers rests on the neophyte to test himself in the real world of the classroom. It gives answers to the student's questions, "Can I teach?" and, "Do I like to teach?". Second, student teaching ideally provides a gradual, somewhat controlled, entrance into classroom teaching. This regulated entrance allows the beginner to take increasing responsibility as he gains increasing mastery. Third, student teaching is the profession's test of competence. While admittedly few fail in student teaching, it does represent a performance test of sorts. Fourth, student teaching is the arena in which the beginner tests out theory and professional knowledge. Fifth, student teaching is normally one of the few opportunities teachers have to receive sustained feedback and analysis of their teaching from both university and school supervisors. It is a high-impact experience and a period of intense learning. However, the intense nature of the student learning experiences makes it a two-edged sword.

After a period of observation and participation, the prospective teacher takes over teaching duties for a number of weeks. The regular teacher becomes the supervising teacher, prescribing the goals of instruction and the actual content to be taught. He is responsible to the school for the student teacher's performance. The effective supervising teacher spends a good deal of time with the student teacher answering questions, suggesting approaches he might try, and generally helping him get acclimated to his new role. Normally, the teacher education supervisor holds seminars and classes during which major problems that have developed during student teaching are analyzed.

As explained and advocated, student teaching is a crucial phase of any teacher education programme. In India, we have a very good student teaching programme supervised by the teacher educators and teachers in the real class rooms.

Hence, the present study is intended to evaluate the effectiveness of student teaching. For this, self-evaluation of teaching is to be carried out by the student teachers.

OBJECTIVE OF THE STUDY

The objectives of the present study entitled "The Role of Self-Evaluation of Lessons by the Prospective Teachers in Enhancing their Teaching Efficiency" are

1. To identify the effectiveness of student teaching,
2. To identify the effectiveness of student teaching in terms of self-evaluation,
3. To identify the merits and limitations of student teaching,
4. To suggest appropriate measures to enhance the teaching effectiveness.

SCOPE OF THE STUDY

Evaluation is a broad concept which involves many things in various fields. The present study is confined to the evaluation of student teaching to identify the limitations and merits of the student teaching. The present study is also confined to the sample of prospective teachers studying in the colleges of Education affiliated to Nagarjuna University. This study also deals only with the evaluation of lessons of prospective teachers, in terms of self-evaluation.

2

REVIEW OF RELATED RESEARCH

IMPORTANCE OF RELATED RESEARCH

Any worthwhile research study in any field of knowledge requires an adequate familiarity with the work which has already been done in the same area. A summary of the writings of recognized authorities and previous research provides evidence that the research is familiar with the what is already known and what is still unknown and untested. Since effective research is based upon past knowledge, this step helps to eliminate the duplication of what has been done, and provides useful hypotheses and helpful suggestions for significant investigations (Best).

Citing studies that show substantial agreement and those that seem to present conflicting conclusions helps to sharpen and define understanding of existing knowledge in the problem area, provides a back ground for the research project, and makes the reader aware of the status of the issue. Parading a long list of annotated studies relating to the problem is ineffective and inappropriate. Only those studies that are plainly relevant, competently executed, and clearly reported should be included.

In searching related literature, the researcher should note certain important elements. They include : 1. Reports of closely related studies that have been investigated, 2. Design of the study, including procedures employed and data-gathering instruments used, 3. Populations that were sampled and sampling methods employed, 4. Variables that were defined, 4. Extraneous variables that could have affected the findings, 6. Faults that could have been avoided, and 7. Recommendations for further research.

RESEARCH STUDIES IN STUDENT TEACHING

Preparation for Student Teaching

Sharma and Kaur found a few and qualitatively poor demonstration lessons in Punjabi language because of the non-school teaching experience of teacher educators. They also found superficial and irrelevant points in discussion lessons. They suggested increasing number of demonstration lessons allowing student teachers to observe a number of good lessons and then deliver not one but 4 or 5 discussion lessons.

Nair and Kulandaivel found that demonstration lessons are useful in student teaching.

Sharma found in U.P. that observation of lessons of school teachers, before practice teaching, was not in practice and demonstration lessons were not delivered in many institutions and some inadequate, and the period of induction was too short specially in affiliated colleges.

Kohli found in Punjabi that 60% of teacher educators favored 2 demonstration lessons, 30% favored 3 lessons and 10% favored 4 lessons. 91.5% of them suggested more than 2 discussion lessons to be given by each student teacher, 93.1% of them suggested demonstration teaching by experienced school teachers.

Pant found that 88% of student teachers felt the need for pre-internship orientation, 70% of them wanted more demonstration lessons. He recommended ten days of pre-internship orientation programme.

Srinivasacharyulu found that student teachers favoured case studies, educational tours and citizenship training camps and suggested provision of demonstration lessons involving varieties of techniques and demonstration lessons to be given by expert school teachers.

Kohli found that there was no pre-intership programme in Punjabi.

Shah and Dasji found that from among 41 Colleges of Education 90% oriented their trainees through demonstration lessons, 51% undertook practice in simulation for orienting their trainees, 46% were satisfied in orientation through a few lectures and 41% provided orientation through classroom lectures. 25% colleges provided model lessons in each of the skills, 44% colleges followed practice of criticism lessons, and 56% colleges employed micro-teaching techniques.

Mohanty did not find proper pre-practice teaching preparation in the colleges of education of Orissa and hence he suggested various measures including more stress on demonstration lessons, audio-visual education and on still training.

Bhaskara Rao recommended that the increase in number in demonstration lessons will increase the efficiency of teaching practice in classroom situations.

Bhaskara Rao stressed the use of micro-teaching teaching techniques both in demonstration lessons and in student practice teaching for teacher effectiveness.

Robertson studied the problem of student teacher and pupil interaction and suggested more classroom observation time not only during student teaching assignment but also prior to it.

Sixty five per cent student teachers found difficulty in preparing unit plans, 75% did not have chance to observe demonstration lessons using illustrative aids, 52% found difficulty in freehand blackboard drawing, 53% did not find completion of teaching of method theory courses before starting of practice teaching (Singh and Nayer). Singh and Nayer suggested provision of demonstration lesson in varieties of methods applicable for teaching method subject(s) and training in unit plans and they also reported that 39% of student teachers had not studied the method subjects taken by them.

Singh experimented on teacher preparation for life-long education on 24 student teachers and gave them practical experience of planning unorthodox lessons with a view to enable pupils to lay hand on tools which help in continuing education. Singh states that experience helped them very much in improving the quality of their practice teaching programmes.

Damodar found lack of training in black board work, and in audio-visual education. The teaching practice criticism lesson proformas were filled in as a formality.

Goel found that no training was being given in training colleges of India for the use of school broadcasts (Buch).

Naly found that the pre-service teaching training programme helped the graduates students to acquire the skills needed to perform most of the 23 teaching skills listed in the questionnaires and the students recommended more opportunities to be provided for observation and short intership and more class time for simulation and solution of problem which occur in teaching situations rather than in educational theory.

Resources for Student Teaching

Lack of proper curriculum for educational technology in the teacher training colleges was found by Patel. There was provision of limited facilities for practical educational technology experiences. The colleges also did not have resources such as audio-visual laboratory, workshop, etc.

Mehrotra did not find adequate use of modern methods of teaching in the teacher training programmes meant for science and mathematics teachers.

Sharma and Kaur pointed out that lack of contact with school teaching experience on the part of members of staff of training colleges resulted in poor quality of demonstration lessons.

Various types of aids found in colleges were film projector 72.5%, filmstrip projector 47.3%, epidiascope 50%, overhead projector 3.1%, films 45.4%, film strops 59.1%, slides 40.9%, models 52.7%, separate audio-visual rooms 34.5%, workshop 4.8%, graphic room 10.9%, photo laboratory 9.1%, auditorium 40%. In case of 33.6% colleges lecturers indication were kept in-charge of audio-visual education an din case of 26.3% colleges services of trained part-time operators were available. On the whole the position of audio visual aids was poor (Aggarwal).

Kohli found that the student teachers of Punjab were not

adequately trained in audiovisual education.

Goel found that only 31% colleges had staff members who were trained in audio-visual education. The percentages of hardwares found in these colleges were tape recorder 94% film strip projector 88%, slide projector 87%, overhead projector 29%, 16 mm film projector 29%, epidiascope 25%, record player 10%, gramophone 4%, 8mm silent film projector 4%, video tape recorder 4%, public address system 2%, linguaphone 2%, and opaque projector 2%.

Libera found an increased demand for use of overhead transparencies, video tapes, computer assisted programmes, 16 mm films, video discs, etc. The respondents considered themselves highly proficient in using A.V. Media.

Stocum found the use of videotape recorders by supervisors as very much effective (Mohanty).

Mallaya found that the library facilities available in the training colleges of Madhya Pradesh were inadequate.

Marker found that Government training colleges of Maharashtra had more resources than the private training colleges.

Kawtra found that one-third of the training colleges subscribed to less than 30 periodicals out of which less than 10 were in education.

Bhaskara Rao found that the colleges of Education in Andhra Pradesh didn't subscribe even for 10 periodicals.

The library facilities in most of teacher education colleges in A.P. are meagre and the books available are also either out-dated or substandard (Bhaskara Rao).

Shukla did not find adequate library facilities in the training colleges of Orissa and he recommended increase in the number of working hours of libraries and for having separate rooms for audio-visual education, having physical education teachers.

Damodar found that most of the training colleges in Andhra Pradesh did not have necessary equipments and accommodation. Nearly one half of the training colleges did not have extension work.

Pant reported the small size of blackboards and poor condition of laboratories and other facilities in schools. He suggested payment of remuneration to co-operating teachers.

Kohli found the necessity of having subject libraries, well equipped science laboratories, well equipped subject rooms, well equipped audio-visual centers. Seven out of fifteen colleges in Punjab did not have science laboratories. He recommended that all training colleges should be residential. He also suggested that members of staff training colleges should be sent on deputation to schools and vice-versa.

Bhaskara Rao opined that the colleges of Education should provide all the necessary resources—such as good libraries, well equipped libraries, qualified teacher educators, proper audio-visual teaching aids, appropriate infrastructural facilities—for student teaching.

Lessons of Student Teaching

Bhaskara Rao did not find any uniformity in fixing the number of practice teaching lessons in different universities of Andhra Pradesh and recommended for a common pattern in the state as well throughout the nation for equal standards.

Joseph did not find uniformity in the number of subjects offered for practice teaching and different items of practical working in the training programmes in Kerala. The respondent staff members suggested practice teaching for a period of 30 days whereas the student teachers suggested for 20-30 days.

Williams, Deever and Flynn in their survey of professional laboratory experiences in Oklahoma found that the number of hours of observation varied between 6-32 hours. They also found that there was a definite criterion for selection of schools and co-operating teachers.

Palsane and Ghanchi found that the number of practice teaching lessons to be delivered by a student teacher was fixed arbitrarily without taking into consideration the needs, abilities and past experiences of individual student teachers.

Shah reported that the number of practice teaching lessons were fixed in India, but not in U.S.A. and U.K.

Brinegar and Schmizzi studied the opinion of 645 Indiana Public School teachers and found that 73% of the respondents favoured student teaching after teaching of method theory courses and 64% favoured full day student teaching for a full semester.

Pant reported that 40% of interns found the programme to be very short and they suggested practice teaching programme of eight weeks.

Bhaskara Rao has informed that he has seen 3 types of teaching practice schedules in his 12 years of teaching experience as a teacher educator. The Nagarjuna University has prescribed 10 lessons for each subject to be taught in student teaching, later increased to 15 lessons for each subject and again modified the number to 13 lessons. He recommends that the authorities shouldn't change the number of lessons concerned to student teaching at frequent intervals on the recommendation of the staff of the affiliated colleges as they recommend as per their will and pleasure. The authorities should give priority to the highest officers of teacher education at these situations.

The University Education Commission (Ministry of Education), Government of India, suggested 12 weeks of supervised school practice and careful selection of schools. The commission criticized the teacher training programmes for giving too little time for school practice and too little weight on assessing the performance of student teachers.

Khanapurkar and Khanapurkar found that student teachers could be effectively involved in organization of school co-curricular activities, maintenance of school records and seeking of parental co-operation during practice teaching programme. They advised that the practice teaching should be in fixed intervals.

Sharma, found hurried practice teaching, non-maintenance of dairies, non-administration of tests, non-participation in various co-curricular activities of practicing schools, and lack of facilities for experience in teaching in various types of schools in U.P.

Shah and Darji found that various types of organizational patterns were in vogue in training colleges of India. Among the respondents, percentages of various patterns were block practice teaching-46%, continuous practice-31%, distributed practice throughout the year-19%, daily pre-noon practice-12%, daily after-noon practice-10%, alternate day practice-7%, and adoption/internship-10%.

Dossey and Brown reported that there was provision of 10

hours of observation of teaching activities and environment, 55 hours of supervised classroom teaching and micro-teaching experiences, and 35 hours of clinical experiences in areas of mathematics teacher education in Illinois state University. The student teachers had content test before admission and their student teaching programme was of 10 weeks duration.

A content Test by name EdCET is there in A.P. to admit students in colleges (Bhaskara Rao).

Damodar found in A.P. that neither the student teachers nor their teachers were taking practice teaching programmes seriously. Some of them treated internship period as vacation and left the headquarters after doing some formalities for the sake of record.

Davis did not find any significant difference between programmes for 8 weeks and programmes for 16 weeks.

Marker found that organisation was better in government training colleges than in private ones in Maharashtra.

Kohli found in Punjab that block practice teaching for a month was a farce, a joke and nothing less than a fraud. Most of the student teachers did not attend schools during the practice teaching period. Insincerity was rampant among both teacher educators and their student teachers even to the extent of violation of university norms and guidelines. He suggested replacement of block teaching practice by comprehensive internship.

Shukla found variations in numbers of practice teaching schools for a college which varied from 2 to 24. Student teachers were permitted to offer a method subject which they had not taken at their graduation stage. Number of methods also varied from college to college. There was no flexibility in the number of lessons to be delivered.

Robertson pointed out the need for the provision of more classroom observation time not only during student teaching but prior to it.

Ganju reported that individual needs, capacities and interests of student teachers were being overlooked.

Srivastava found variations in marks allotted for student teaching, number of lessons to be delivered and amount of time spent for

Singh prepared student teachers for life long education and their practice teaching lessons were based on lifelong education strategies which include teaching to consult dictionary, teaching use of index, teaching in a language laboratory, teaching preparing bibliography, map reading, pupil teaching other pupils, teaching through gramophone, radio listening, student teachers becoming learners, use of strip projectors, student teachers becoming learners. Use of these activities were very much appreciated by teachers of concerned co-operation schools.

Singh and Nayer found that 80% of student teachers felt that employing new methods of teaching in practice teaching programmes hampered completion of school courses.

Naidu found that student teachers of Andhra Pradesh did not bother about specific methdos or teaching aids during their practice teaching programmes.

Sukhia found the use of Herbartian steps of lesson planning by the student teachers in their practice teaching lesson plans and also found that classes of supervisor's choice were being imposed on the student teachers.

Srinivasacharyulu suggested to give stress to co-curricular activities of schools.

Jones suggested to give more emphasis on helping interns to become acquainted with local and community problems. Participation in a wide-variety of administrative tasks and extra-curricular activities were also suggested by him.

In Naly's survey, the graduates suggested for providing opportunities for teaching experience in different methods, organizing orientation programmes before admission and devoting more time for simulating and solving classroom teaching problems.

A.I.T.E. suggested in-class activities in varieties of situations such as with or without sufficient equipment, with children of different levels, with heterogeneous/homogeneous groups, and with urban/rural pupils.

Assessment of Student Teaching

Banerjee found that practice teaching was worst hit aspect in the examination of teacher trainees of 1954-55 session of the

Government Central Pedagogical Institute, Allahabad.

Palsane and Ghanchi reported lack of continuous and integrated evaluation practices in 62 Colleges of Education.

Mallaya found defective evaluation techniques and large variations in internal and external assessments in Assam.

Singh and Kaur (1970) found that the evaluation programmes did not consider the aspects of Punjabi language student teaching such as speech training, preparation of teaching aids, blackboard work, hand writing, phonetics, organization of literary activities. They recommended that the evaluation of classroom teaching performance be based at least on performances in three lessons instead of one lesson and also recommended to improve the techniques of evaluation.

Srivastava reported that the majority of teacher educators of the Central Institute of Education were not satisfied with the prevailing evaluation practices. There were variations in award of marks.

Morris and Stines did not find any uniform and written criteria of evaluation in U.K. In case of majority of colleges final gradings were given in staff meetings and border-line cases were adjudicated by external examiners.

According to ten ace educationists of India, the evaluation of student teaching was defective (Rai). It often did not have a set criteria. It was not objective systematic and pin-pointed. It was based mostly on partial observation of one or two lessons.

Cohen referred to the need for serious examination of the concept of college supervisors as a reliable and valid source of evaluation.

Carter reported deficiencies in evaluation procedures for student teachers used in the teacher education curriculum of University of South Carilina at Aiken.

Marr, et al, pointed in out in reference to three colleges of Education in Punjab the need for having a continuous system of evaluation. They also found that most of the old examiners were out of contact with the newer developments in teaching techniques.

Joshi pointed out, based on 3 case studies, the necessity for having a criteria of evaluation.

DEPSE suggested that not more than two lessons were to be evaluated in a normal classroom period.

Willian, Deever and flynn found an effective system of continuous evaluation in teacher training programme of Oklahoma.

Wilkinson, found that the factors that influenced classroom behaviours of student teacher were grade level and socio-economic level of school students and the preference of a student teacher for a particular age group of school students.

Das found through the study of B.Ed. Programme in Hoogly a positive correlation between university theory and practical marks. He also found that internal examiner's opinion was repeated at the time of final evaluation of student teaching.

Damodar found better results in practicals than in theory at marks of student teachers of training colleges of Andhra Pradesh. He recommended joint evaluation by schools and colleges.

Sharma found that nearly 98% of teacher educators were in favour in internal evaluation in Utter Pradesh. He also found that nearly 58% of teacher educators felt that the evaluation was biased.

Sharma found low correlation between theory and practical marks of B.Ed. students of a college of education affiliated to Punjab University.

Bourai did not find any positive correlation between theory and practical marks of B.Ed. student teachers of a teacher training college in Rajasthan.

Gupta found that student teachers of Punjab did better in practicals than in theory. 99% of them got first division in teaching whereas only 23% got first division in theory.

Dosajh found great disparity between weightages given to teaching skills by various respondents. There was also low correlation between the assessment made by the lecturers and the school teachers.

Devi pointed out the need for giving equal weightage to internal and external assessments.

The University Education commission reported that student teachers never failed in their practical tests.

Shukla found poor quality of evaluation of student teaching in the teacher training colleges of Orissa. The criteria of evaluation differed even among colleges situated under provision of 25% internal evaluation in case of the Regional college of Education now Regional Institute of Education, Bhubaneswar whereas there was the provision of 10% internal evaluation in case of other colleges affiliated to the same university. The school staff participated in evaluation in case of the former, which was not so in case of the later. He recommended 150 marks for internal and 150 marks for external evaluation of teaching practice, and marks internal and 50 marks external evaluation for the 5 practical assignments.

Shah and Darji found practice of both internal and external examiner evaluation in 54% colleges, only internal examiner evaluation in 37% colleges and only external examiner evaluation in 5% colleges. In case of 93% colleges final evaluation was done by a team of examiners. There was a proforma for evaluation in case of 54 colleges.

Howey, Yarger and Joyce found that evaluation of student teaching in U.S.A., in most of the cases, was jointly done by the school and the college. In case of 40% of the institutions self-evaluation by the student teachers was also in practice.

Patel found that experienced student teachers did better than the fresh ones.

Bhaskara Rao found that highly qualified pre-service teachers were more confident about their teaching, but showed a little bit negligence. The undergraduate pre-service teaching were sincere in their attempts as many of them wanted to become teachers.

Joseph found that the student teachers showed greater confidence in the capacity of school staff for evaluation.

Tudhope found agreement between final teaching marks and the future success of student teachers in the teaching profession. But, Wiseman and Start did not find any correlation between final teaching grades and the future success in the teaching profession.

Rachal studied the question of student teacher effectiveness in the summative self-evaluation of teaching competencies on a sample of 131 student teachers and found that the student teachers failed to predict their teaching strengths and weaknesses. An instructional sequence combined with the self-evaluation of videotaped teaching performance did not aid in improving the student teacher effectiveness in the self-evaluation of teaching competencies (Mohanty).

Pangotra found that final teaching marks of 80 trained graduate teachers having 2 to 5 years of teaching experience and teaching English, Social Studies, General Science and Mathematics subjects had low but significant correlation at 0.1 level with the ratings of headmasters and low and insignificant correlation with the results of the subjects taught by them. He suggested for evolving criteria of evaluation, replacement of external examination by internal examination and making the scope of evaluation broader by taking into consideration aspects such as the ability in diagnosing difficulties of school students, ability in developing remedial programmes, ability in management of classrooms, ability in organization and arrangement of subject matter, attitude towards teaching profession, teacher-student relationship, and personality characteristics of student teachers.

Desmukh and Nagoshe suggested a tool for assessment of student teaching. The aspects to be assessed were lesson planning 20% classroom interaction 70% and teacher's personality 10%. Lesson plan consisted of clarity of objectives and specifications, appropriateness of contents, logical organization of learning experiences, and appropriateness of form of lessons. Class interaction consisted of appropriateness and effective use of methods and teaching techniques, command over subject matter, effective use of teaching aids, creation of conducive climate for learning, preparation of students, and realization of objectives. Teachers personality consisted of appearance, voice, confidence, manners, resourcefulness, and imagination.

Supervision and Guidance in Student Teaching

Rai found that supervision of student teaching was very much defective, and it was a more formality and also it was mechanical, arbitrary, subjective, negative, not constructive, less developmental, more static and stereo-typed.

Carter reported deficiencies in the areas of personnel for supervision in the teacher education curriculum.

Stocum found that most of the supervisors used a observation instrument developed by the college/university of themselves or developed a specific instrument to meet individual needs. Most of the supervisors indicated that they usually held post observation conferences and less than one half of the supervisors held pre-observation conferences.

Shukla found that the amount of lessons supervised by staff members was comparatively much less (10%) in case of Regional College of Education, Bhubaneswar than that found in case of other teacher training colleges or Orissa. In the former college, school teachers were involved in supervision work. He suggested supervision to be done by a faculty member or by a teacher who has competence both in content and pedagogy.

Bhaskara Rao found that three lessons were supervised by teacher educators and 7-10 lessons by school teachers where the teachers were undergoing internship.

Kohli found in Punjab that practice teaching lessons were supervised by staff members who had not specialized in concerned content areas.

Sukhia found too much distance between the supervisors and the student teachers. A lesson of 40 minutes duration was being observed by supervisors for nearly 8 minutes only.

Cope found that teacher educators who did not have any school experience faced difficulties in supervising practice lessons.

In India, except two to five percent, all the teacher educators were not having any school teaching experience (Bhaskara Rao). They also did not show any interest to teach in schools for some time even after they became makers of teachers.

Kay found that the college supervisors often did not define their remarks objectively and did not make their judgments over.

Griffiths and Moore found that school heads and their teachers lacked in expertise required of a supervisor.

Joseph found that student teachers of Kerala state showed

greater amount of confidence in the capacity of school staff for supervision. This view was not shared by staff members of colleges of education.

Wilkinson surveyed the reports of supervisors and found that they neglected specific classroom behaviours of student teachers and did not specifically point out their strengths and weaknesses.

Johnson found that the student teachers moved towards dogmatism of their supervisions.

The number of student teachers supervised by a supervisor varied from 8 to 24 (Second National Survey of Secondary Teacher Education in India).

Bourai found, in a college in Rajasthan, that no importance had been given to objectives of lessons, design of lessons, ending of lessons, and content preparation.

The University Education commission suggested that there was no need for supervisors to observe each lesson.

Srinivasacharyulu found that student teachers did not favour pointing out of their mistakes by the concerned supervisors in front of school students.

Singh and Nayer found that 53% of them did not get adequate guidance in preparation of content, 65% of them did not get adequate guidance in preparation of aids, 37% of them did not get any help from their supervisors, and 37% of them hesitated to discuss their problems with the supervisors.

Rastogi, in a study of supervision of practice teaching programme of correspondence course student teachers, found average number of remarks per lesson by school principals was 3.5 in comparison to 8.5 by the staff members of the Central Institute of Education. He also found predominance of appreciative remarks in the observations made by the school principals.

Bourai found that the supervisory remarks were given superficially and they gave less stress on the methods of teaching and knowledge of the subject matter. Irrelevant remarks such as 'subject matter dull', 'upto the mark', 'blackboard writing neat and clean', 'method needs improvement', 'charming personality', etc., were found.

Benniw found that student teachers received more amount of help from their campus supervisors than from their classroom co-operating teachers.

Trimmer found that only 10% of student teachers were satisfied with the guidance provided by co-operating teachers. The student teachers pointed out defects such as lack of instructive criticism, and flock of holding of regular feedback conferences and they suggested that opportunities may be provided to them during student teaching programmes so they may be able to teach for certain periods without anyone observing them. They also, pointed out the need for careful selection of co-operating teachers and organization of special training programmes for them so as to improve the standard of their ability of supervision.

Price found that supervising teachers influenced the behaviours of student teachers assigned to them.

Copeland pointed out the need for adequate training to the mentors of student teaching.

Marlow Ediger felt that mentor teachers are the key persons in teacher education.

Hardy found that the co-operating teachers had significant influence on the concerns of student teachers.

Smith found that in-service programmes were very much helpful in clarifying roles of co-operating teachers and student teachers.

Reading and Bloom found that team supervision of student teaching with the team members as 1 teacher, 1 or 2 classroom teachers and 2 or 3 student teachers were very much effective.

Efron found seminar to be more effective strategy than normal supervision or supply of handbook and written suggestions in student teaching programme.

Joshi found the usefulness of having criteria for analyzing the performances of student teachers.

Haamujompa recommended that supervision should adopt clinical model and should be based on scientific and democratic approaches. Co-operating teachers were to guide the student teacher in observing classes, in planning, in independent teaching and in understanding pupils. The student teachers were to be acquainted with professional organizations. The conferences were to be made as effective learning experiences.

Khanapurkar and Khanapurkar found practices such as correction of lesson plans prior to delivery of lessons, conveying reactions of individual supervisors over lessons to the concerned method teachers, organization of weekend staff cönferences concerning practice teaching, and involvement of school teachers in supervision, were found to be very much useful.

Monson and Bebb found that in-service training seminars with student teaching supervisors on each Thursday morning for ten weeks were favoured by supervisors as well as student teachers. The topics covered under the in-service training seminars were planning and expectation of roles, conferencing and role playing, establishing effective personal, and working relationships, goal setting and behavioral objectives, observing behaviours and recording of observation, questioning and measuring pupil attention, self-assessment-helping student teacher assess themselves, developing bases for evaluation- verbal and non-verbal interaction analysis, and evaluating student teacher progress.

Innovations in Student Teaching

Damodar did not find use of innovations in student teaching such as micro-teaching and training in simulation in A.P. in 1986. But, micro-teaching is now a part of teacher education in Andhra Pradesh (Bhaskara Rao).

Joshi found that in teacher training institutions there was negligible attempt for use of innovations such as micro-teaching, programmed learning, interaction analysis, and self-learning projects. Block teaching practice was reported as innovation for one teacher training colleges. Factors of resistance to innovations were lack of facilities, lack of funds, lack of time to pursue new ideas, lack of professional guidance, lack of support from education departments.

The Canadian Teachers Federation found that innovative practices were in vogue in 50% teacher education institutions of Canada. Various innovative practices in use in Canada were use of over head projector 89% use of video tape recorder 74%, use of group discussion techniques 89% micro teaching mini course and interaction analysis 53%, and school faculty committees on practice teaching 52%.

Joshi found that acceptance of innovations depended on factors such as awareness, leadership service, support, interest, problem solving approach, system innovativeness, prestige value, and intrinsic value. Resistance to innovations depended on factors such as lack of physical facilities, lack of service, lack of support, rigid framework, inter-personal disharmony, leadership crisis, personality crisis, and over work.

Sukhia reported that the supervisors of student teaching programmes seemed to be averse to the innovations in teaching and improving their own teaching expertise through research techniques.

Bone (1980) reported that final year graduate students has been working in school on a part time basis, on payment of salary. The school teachers had been also involved in teaching work in University of British Columbia. The student teachers had been also involved in their self-assessment towards the middle of the programme.

Buch made case studies of innovations in three teacher education institutions. The study on the programmes of the Department of Education of the M.S. University of Baroda, pointed out that innovations were undertaken in 1. Pre-practice teaching preparation—micro-teaching and 2. evaluation -transfer of power from external to internal and making whole evaluation process a continuous one. The study on the programmes of the Gandhi Shikshan Bhavan, Bombay reported innovations such as development of self-study and group-study methods, activity-centered learning, helping school in solving their problems, development of a curriculum for lifelong education. Such innovations led to development of more favourable attitude at least among 20% student teachers of 1970-74 periods.

The study on the programmes of linking teacher education to the needs of community at the M.B. Patel College of Education, Sardar Patel University, Vallabh Vidyanagar reported innovations such as visits to rural sites, arrangement of extra-mural lectures in rural areas, and symposia and discussions on rural sociology (Buch).

Buch reported development of skills of instruction through micro-teaching and simulation at the Center of Advanced Study in Education, M.S. University of Baroda. In this programme a trainee used to give at-least 3 cycles of micro-lessons with a group of 6 to 7 peers as students and the skills covered were stimulus variation, probing questioning, reinforcement, illustrating with examples, and explaining (APEID).

Buch reported the following innovations in teacher education at the M.S. University of Baroda. They were 1. semester system, 2. micro-teaching, 3. interaction analysis, 4. preparation of instructional and lesson plans, 5. observation of classroom teaching, 6. preparation of indigenous teaching aids, 7. evaluation of lesson, 8. preparation of socio-grams and their interpretation, 9. performing classroom experiments in role playing and goal setting behavior in game situation, 10. demonstration of the effects of failure cues and success cues on learning through help giving behaviour, 11. preparation of case study of a child showing problem behaviour, 12. practical work involving administering and scoring of different types of psychological and educational tests, 13. preparing a profile of a student for guidance purposes, 14. practical work leading to the preparation of pupils, progress card and cumulative record card. 15. practical work in writing instructional objectives in behavioural terms, 16. preparing objectives based items, 17. preparing unit tests 18. preparing model question papers, 19. practical work in organizing Parent Teacher Association meetings, Health exhibitions, etc., 20. practical work to develop skills in preparing a class time-table, home-work time-table, etc., 21. preparing out lines of educational projects, and 22. preparing different types of assignments (APEID).

Buch and Buch and Sansanwal reported innovations in teacher preparation programme at Vidya Bhavan G.S. Teachers College, Udayapur, which were 1. open air session, wherein the whole institution moved to one of the rural areas for a period of several days to inculcate self-reliance in student teachers and to acquaint with them the way of life of the rural people and during this period besides participation in community living activities, the student teachers surveyed localities, organized functions and exhibitions, 2. block teaching practice in schools situated within a radius of 100 miles, wherein 20 student teachers were attached to one staff member for a fortnight and the practice teaching activities included items such as classroom teaching, maintenance of school records, participation in running the school, study of home environment of the school children, development of skills in teaching in a rural environment, devising educational activities, preparing teaching aids, studying relation of the community with the school, etc. (APEID).

Buch and Mukhopadhyay reported the programme of training teachers for their roles as rural reconstruction workers at Gandhi Vidyapeeth, Vechi, Gujarat. The trainees undertook activities such as agricultural and spinning work, besides getting practice in other teaching and non-teaching activities of a teacher. During practice teaching period, they participated in daily assemblies, sports, sanitation, craft work, school community kitchen activities. They also took classes for one work project on a subsidiary craft such as preparing candles, hair oils, chalk sticks, dusters of herbal medicines. Non-classroom teaching activities were done at three places-1. activities at schools consisted of gardening, wall newspaper, exhibitions, children's journals assignments, question boxes, self-service co-operative shop, parent teacher association, sports, music, dance, drama, cultural activities, teachers, discussions, flag hoisting ceremony, national songs and case studies of children, 2. activities at homes included decorating the houses for scientific ways of living, discussion with parents help in farm work, first aid and barefoot doctor's work, sanitary work - constructing simple but better latrines, bath rooms, disposal of waste, hygienic ways of living, compost pits, manual or gas plants, preparing spinning wheels, and servicing, 3. activities in society included- organizing community meetings, village sanitation, prayer meetings, youth clubs, social education, child education, play centers, work camps (Shramadan Sibirs), surveying sanitation training. Crash programme on agricultural was another important activity. Lessons were distributed among primary, primary—basic secondary and post—basic schools (APEID).

Buch and Sharma reported innovation at Mouni Vidyapith, Gargoti. It was on teacher education in rural setting. The programme had an intimate school-college coordination. Vidyapith's teachers visited the schools periodically and organized demonstration teaching in them. The teachers of the schools also were invited to the Vidyapith for getting training on audio-visual education. There were provisions for preparation of common teaching aids for rural schools, training in parent-school co-operation training, in conducting social education classes, and study of the problems of wastage and stagnation (APEID).

Buch and Roy reported innovation at Gujarat Vidyapeeth, Ahmadabad. The innovation was the programme of linking teacher education with rural reconstruction. It consisted of observation of 60 lessons, delivery of 10 lessons in attached experimental basic school, delivery of remaining 20 lessons in other schools (mostly rural schools) during internship programme, training in craft, community living in hostel and off-campus programmes in rural areas. Off-campus programmes were organized in six rural service extension centers or in any post-basic school in the rural area. The student teachers participated in different types of social works (APEID).

Buch, Yadav, Joshi and Mukhopadhyay reported on innovations in teacher education for relating education to life in an urban setting and to rural uplift. The Gandhi Shikshan Bhavan, Bombay had adopted innovations such as 1. self study method to develop self-reliance, confidence, concentration, comprehension, curiosity, proper method of taking down points, method of answering orally in a precise way and habit of correcting others without hurting them through techniques such as oral questions and answers, reading of material, essay type tests, use of library, atlas, laboratory apparatus, etc., 2. group study methods - to develop team spirit, co-operation, leadership confidence, self-reliance, respect for others' views, concise method of presentation, proper method of discussion and habit of drawing up one's own notes and points through techniques such as group activity with each group having a leader, working on a different theme, submitting report, reading and discussing them, 3. activity lessons - to find use for waste, to be economical in money, time and space, to develop aesthetic sense, to learn to be neat and tidy, to develop necessary skills and to learn to be proud of them through techniques such as preparation of models, charts, folders, albums, herbariums, dress in certain periods of history, cleaning work, measurement of actual distance, self performed experiments, map drawing in class, planing and division of work, collection of materials and tools, working together in class, completing the work in time, 4. dramatization - to develop comprehension, writing skills, proper audience reaction, understanding life through characters, time and place, appreciation of abilities and feelings of others and self-criticism through techniques such as complete study of the subject, re-writing in the form of a play, selection of actors, a little practice, stitching of the dresses, setting, staging, acting and criticism by actors, audience, director and judges, 5. organization of programmes - for development of emotional integration, national and international brotherhood, organizational ability, team spirit, enthusiasm for democratic living, qualities of leadership and frugal habits, collection and saving of money through techniques such as observation of festivals, national days, birth days of great men, talks by actual men from actual fields-freedom fighters, writers, poets, scientists, foreigners, parents, picnics, visits, bhajans, cleanliness campaigns, exhibitions, bulletin board maintenance, organization of matches, sports, etc., 6. social service-consisting of activities such as literacy programmes community health services, moral science and recreational activities. The innovations at M.B. Patel college of Education, Vallabh Vidyanagar included 1. orientation on problems of rural areas- through visits to rural places, extra mural lectures, symposia and discussions on rural sociology and economics led by experts in those fields, 2. community programme - in summer for students of rural communities, 3. school-college co-operation through 10 out post centers, one such center covering 20 to 25 schools, 4. school adoption, where in 10 to 12 schools were adopted each year and these schools were supplied with teaching aids (APEID).

UNESCO mentions various innovative practices used in preparation of educational personnel. This information was compiled from the questionnaire returned by 426 institutions located in 104 countries. Out of these institutions, there were 19 institutions from India which were involved in preparation of secondary school teachers. Various innovative practices in vogue in these Indian institutions were 1. micro-teaching, 2. block teaching practice, 3. unit plan, 4. use of audio-visual materials, 5. searching interviews, 6. model writing practices, 7. model reading practices, 8. preparation of improvised aids, 9. games and sports 10. drama, music and cultural functions, 11. Debates and symposia, 12. music adoption of village for development, 13 survey, 14. manual work for rural development, 15. functional literacy, 16. remedial teaching 17. programmed learning, 18. macro-teaching, 19. maintenance of diary, 20. morning condition classes and training in nature cure, 21. weekly lectures on saints and sages of eminence, 22. making film strips, 23. improvisation of chemistry kit for rural high schools, 24. community work, 25. programme for low achieving student teachers, 26. use of 10 point criteria for evaluation. 27. physical science clubs, 28.

seminary, 29. history room, 30. health project, 31. school adoption, 32. mid term demonstration lesson, 33. pre-teaching demonstration lesson, 34. discussion on student teaching, 35. adoption of a village, 36. tutorials, 37. subject associations 38. assessment of total personality. The international scene was different. Out of 426 institutions in all, 306 institutions dealt with secondary teacher preparation. Various innovative practices carried out in these institutions were 1. co-ordination with Public school systems 72 (23.5%), 2. Microteaching 64 (20.9%), 3. student evaluation was conducted by instructors and practitioners - 61 (9.9%), 4. association with and or operates an off-campus training center 54 (17.6%), 5. instructional models 42 (13.7%), 6. individualised instruction 42 (13.7%), 7. Videotaping of teaching 41 (13.4%), 8. team teaching 38 (12.4%), 9. has a curriculum materials laboratory 38 (12.4%), 10. teacher education programme adapted to rural areas 33 (10.8%), 11. programme adapted to urban areas 32 (10.5%), 12. utilizes advanced students as tutors 29 (9.5%), 13. provides courses based on individual needs 28 (9.2%), 14. interaction analysis 28 (9.2%), 15. programme based on minority group and or ethnically different groups 28(9.2%), 16. micro counselling 23 (7.5%), 17 conduct of systematic follow-up studies on recent graduates and participation of former students in evaluation of programmes 22 (7.2%), 18 simulation 22 (7.2%), 19. peer instruction 22 (7.2%), 20. sensitivity training 19 (6.2%), 21. competency/performance-based teacher education programme 18 (5.8%), 22. programmed instruction 17(5.6%), 23. instructional television 17 (5.6%), 24. availability of a manual or printed policy statement of EPP Programme in operational terms 16 (5.2%), 25. graduation criteria other than instructor's marks or grading 15 (4.9%). The innovative practices carried out in 10 (3.3%) institutions were outside educators participate in student evaluation, programme based on under privileged group, and programme on a non-subject matter basis. The programme undertaken in 9 (2.9%) institutions was field experience, programmes undertaken in 6 (2%) institutions were systematic collection of data on student performance, award of certificates/diplomas on completion of an innovative programme, and community education/development activities. Programme undertaken in 5 (1.6%) institutions is internship. Programmes undertaken in 4 (1.3%) institutions were audio-visual laboratory, and early public school experience. Programmes undertaken in 3 (0.9%) institutions were audio-visual techniques and preparation of improvised aids, laboratory of Psychometry, credit system training for community school, CCTV, computer based instruction, and open area teaching. Programmes undertaken in 2 (0.7%) institutions were films, educational road cost-radio, remedial teaching programme, action research, working with small groups of children/special need children, tutorial, native teacher education, block teaching practice, and student teaching in foreign countries. The programmes carried out in 1 (0.3%) institution were 1. adult education, 2. foreign language laboratory, 3. evaluation by inspectors and headmasters, 4. participation in the development of social institutions that contribute to education, 5. full time supervisor of student teaching, 6. preparation and application of various kinds of tests, 7. student voluntary community service activities, 8. mid-year intake of the programme, 9. short term exchanges between teaching staff in schools and colleges in theory and practice, 10. integrated library services, 11. block teaching followed by tutorials 12. workshop/seminar at inter-school and inter-college level, 13. guidance and counselling programme, 14. consultation programme with associated schools, 15. population education, 16. study of methodology used in field by students, 17. display center for scientific experiments, 18. programme stressing on hill tribes, 19. rural development club, 20. a week of intensive practice, 21. project work, 22. problem solving techniques, 23. base knowledge transfer, 24. student team, 25. development of scientific and reading kits for rural schools, 26. internship exchange teachers, 27. self-evaluation, 28. direct teaching methods, 29. learning laboratory, 30. permanent evaluation, 31. integrated internship for theory and practice, 32. unit plan, 33. searching interview, 34. model writing practice, 35. model reading practices, 36. games and sports, 37. drama, music and cultural functions, 38. adoption of village, 39. survey, 40. manual work of rural development, 41. functional literacy, 42. programme for low achieving student teachers, 43. macro-teaching, 44. maintenance of diary, 45. morning condition classes and nature cure, 46. weekly lectures on saints and sages of eminence, 47. making of film strips, 48. improvisation of chemistry kits for rural high schools. 49. use of 10 point criteria for evaluation, 50. physical science club, 51. history room, 52. health project, 53. seminar, 54. school adoption, 55. mid-term demonstration lesson, 56. pre-teaching demonstration lesson, 57. discussion in student teaching, 58. village participation, 59. subject association, 60. assessment of total personality, 61. student teaching on other cultures inside a country, and 62. extended use of educational technology.

3

DESIGN OF RESEARCH

Research design decides the fate of any research proposal and its outcome. As much it is regarded as the heart of any research designing provides a picture for the whole study before starting the work. It is, in a simple language, a plan of action. It is, therefore, desirable to have a methodically designed research plan. So, the following aspects of the research design have been discussed in detail.

The operational definitions of different terms used, the various hypotheses that were framed for verification and the rationale of these syntheses have been discussed.

The sampling techniques selected, the reasons for selection of a particular sampling technique, and the selection of sample according to different variables have also been discussed.

The selection of suitable.tool for the collection of data, and the procedure followed in administering the tool to collect the data required for the present study have also been explained.

OPERATIONAL DEFINITIONS OF KEY TERMS

The operational definitions of the important terms used in the present study are discussed and defined herewith.

Teaching

Teaching is a social and professional activity. It is a process of development. Teaching is a system of actions which induce learning through interpersonal relationship.

Teaching is a purposeful activity. The ultimate goal of teaching is to bring all-round development in a child. The knowledge and practice which help in realizing the goals is the content matter of teaching technology.

Teaching is an art as well as a science because teaching can be studied objectively and scientifically. Teaching has a scientific foundation. This has evolved the concept of teaching technology. Silverman has termed it as constructive educational technology.

Teaching technology is an application of philosophical, sociological and scientific knowledge to teaching for achieving some specific learning objectives.

The content of technology of teaching is based on the following assumptions : 1. Teaching is a scientific process. 2. The desired learning may be generated with the help of appropriate teaching situations. 3. A close relationship may be established between teaching and learning. 4. The teaching activities can be modified and improved. 5. Teaching skills can be developed with the help of feedback devices. 6. The learning objectives may be achieved by performing teaching activities.

The technology of teaching also involves the following assumptions : 1. The content matter can be divided into its elements and each element can be presented independently. 2. The external learning conditions can be created by arranging the elements in a logical sequence. 3. The appropriate reinforcement can be provided continuously by the use of instruction. 4. The student can learn according to his needs and rate of learning. 5. The strategies and tactics of instruction can be used for achieving certain well defined set of instructional objectives. 6. The student can learn successfully without the physical presence of a teacher.

Davies and Robert have developed the content of technology of teaching and classified it into four elements. The following four steps present the structure of the content. 1. Planning of Teaching: The first step includes content analysis, identification of objectives and writing objectives in behavioural terms. 2. Organization of Teaching: The second step consists of teaching strategies and tactics for achieving the objectives of teaching. The rules of instruction are identified under this step. 3. Leading for Teaching: In the third step appropriate communication strategies of teaching are identified. The techniques of motivation are employed for leading the behaviour of the students. The knowledge regarding rapport between teacher and student is considered under this step. 4. Controlling of Teaching: The last step concerns with evaluation of teaching. The main focus of this step is to assess the learning objectives in terms of students' performance. The decision is taken about the realization of teaching objectives. The learners' performance provides the basis to the feedback for teachers and students.

Thus, teaching is a purposeful activity to achieve the objectives of teaching and learning.

Lesson

Perhaps the most useful way to think about instructional functions is in the context of a lesson, the basic unit of instruction. If a lesson is an atom, instructional functions are the sub-atomic particles. A lesson also is composed of the material in a given area of the curriculum to be covered by a teacher and a group of students during one sitting.

Madeline Hunter and her colleagues have probably taught more teachers about good lesson design than any other group of educators. In her programme which is known by a variety of names including Mastery Teaching and Instructional Theory into Practice, Hunter advocates a nine part lesson design. To conduct the prescribed lesson a teacher 1. Provides an anticipatory set for learners, 2. States the objectives of the lesson to learners, 3. States the purpose of the lesson to learners, 4. Provides input to learners, 5. Provides modelling for learners, 6. Checks learners for understanding, 7. Plans guided practice for learners, 8. Achieves closure, and 9. Plans independent practice by learners.

To understand the components of a Hunter-style lesson it may be helpful to think of an actual lesson. Assume you are being taught about the principles of good instruction. Initially, the teacher attempts to involve you in the lesson and prepares you for what is to come (the anticipatory set). To accomplish this function, the teacher asks you to recall a favourite teacher in the past (Sound familiar?). Once your attention is to understand the principles of good instruction and that the specific purpose of today's lesson is to prepare you to select an instructional model to use next week when you commence practice teaching, you will understand your need. Having completed the preliminaries, the teacher begins presenting various principles of good instruction. These include such ideas as reinforcing students for appropriate behaviours and breaking down complex learning activities into simple tasks. As the teacher introduces the principles, he or she also models them whenever possible, thereby giving you concrete examples to remember. Periodically you are asked questions to determine whether you understand what is being taught. The teacher is careful to address questions to all students. Following the introduction of material on the principles of instruction, the teacher gives the prospective teachers an opportunity to practice the principles. The prospective teachers might, for example, conduct a mini-lesson for their classmates in which they use several principles of instruction or they could watch a videotape of a lesson and identify various principles of practice. The teacher then reviews what the prospective teachers were supposed to have accomplished in today's lesson (closure) and assigns home work (indepen dent practice) related to the lesson.

The Hunter format for a lesson arranges instructional functions in such a way that students are likely to be able to use what they learn. It is a format well-suited t8 basic skill development. Other formats may be more appropriate for content based lessons or lessons emphasizing higher-order thinking. The determination of what lesson format use also may be influenced by the choice of an instructional model.

Evaluation

In general, it would seem preparable to reserve the term educational evaluation for application to abstract entities such as programmes, curricula, and organizational variables. Its use implies a general weighing of the value or worth of something, and, as Scriven pointed out it usually involves making comparison to other programmes, curricula or organizational schemes.

There are several definitions of educational evaluation. They differ in level of abstraction and often reflect the specific concerns of the person who formulated them. Perhaps the most extended definition of evaluation has been supplied by Beeby, who described evaluation as "the systematic collection and interpretation of evidence; leading, as part of the process, to a judgement of value with a view to action". The use of the term systematic here implies that what information is needed will be defined with some degree of precision and that efforts to secure such information will be planned. Information gathered by mean of observational procedures, questionnaires, and interviews can contribute to an evaluation enterprise. The important point is that whatever kind of information is gathered should be acquired in a systematic way. This information goes for proper evaluation to derive conclusions and to suggest ways and means.

Prospective Teacher

The students of B.Ed. course, who are undergoing teacher training, are prospective teachers.

Teaching Efficiency

Teaching is an art and a science. The ultimate aim of teaching is to make the students understand what the teacher intends to teach. Perfectness in teaching will be there if there happens a mutual balance between the teacher and the taught in the subject matter. This perfectness is the teaching efficiency.

VARIABLES OF THE STUDY

Variables are intended to see the difference among different factors associated with the study under consideration. The following variables have been considered for the present study as these have a direct impact on the teaching efficiency.

Men versus Women Prospective Teachers

As the psychological and physiological conditions, exposure to society, education and other aspects of men and women vary significantly, these factors will play a role on the teaching efficiency of prospective teachers. Hence sex was taken as a variable to see the difference that exists in men and women teachers.

English versus Telugu Medium Prospective Teachers

Many people think that the children who communicate in their mother tongue or native language will express their opinions and feelings very effectively. This will be same in case of teaching also. So, language was taken as a variable to see the difference in teaching efficiency between English medium teachers and Telugu medium teachers.

Aided versus Un-aided College Trained Prospective Teachers.

To logic, the aided college staff members may have full job satisfaction because of the monitory and other facilities that they enjoy. When one has job satisfaction he may be providing all the conducive training facilities to the student teachers. So, the student teachers who are undergoing training in aided colleges of education may be more efficient than their counter parts getting training in un-aided colleges of education. Hence this variable was taken to study the difference in teaching efficiency between the prospective teachers of aided and un-aided colleges of education.

HYPOTHESES OF THE STUDY

Hypothesis is a pre-conclusion of a phenomena to be verified in real situations collecting the necessary evidence. As the present study is intended to study the merits and limitations of the teaching of prospective teachers in terms of self evaluation the following hypotheses were formulated.

Hypothesis 1

The prospective teachers will have greater satisfaction about their teaching.

Hypothesis 2

There will be a significant difference in the teaching efficiency between the men and women prospective teachers.

Hypothesis 3

There will be a significant difference in the teaching efficiency between the English and Telugu medium prospective teachers.

Hypothesis 4

There will be a significant difference in the teaching efficiency between the prospective teachers studying in aided and unaided colleges of education.

SAMPLE OF THE STUDY

After finalizing the hypotheses of the present study, consideration was given to whether the entire population is to be made the subject for data collection or a particular group is to be selected as representative of the whole population. The entire population here refers to the prospective teachers studying in the Colleges of Education affiliated to Nagarjuna University.

In any research, various methods are utilized for selection of samples. After a detailed study of all these methods and considering the objectives and hypotheses selected for the study, the 'cluster sampling technique' was found to be most suitable for this study.

Cluster sampling involves division of the population of el ementary units under consideration into groups or clusters that serve as primary sampling units (Aggarwal). A selection of the clusters is then made to take up the sample. Thus cluster sampling contains groups of elements instead of individual members or items in the population. For the present study, two clusters were taken, namely, R.V.R. college of Education and A. L. College of Education. The prospective teachers were the primary units.

TOOL OF THE STUDY

A research tool plays a major role in any worthwhile research as it is the sole factor in determining the sound data and in arriving at perfect conclusions about the problem or study in hand, which, ultimately, helps in providing suitable remedial measures to the problem concerned.

The selection and use of tools can be done in to ways. The first one is to construct a tool independently by the investigator for his own study. Here there are many problems in doing so. On preparation and standardization of a perfect tool, Anand and Padma felt that 'A note of caution has to be struck when a researcher develops a tool for his study by merely pooling some items and does not subject it to the sophisticated techniques of tool construction, the result would be then obvious, a poor quality research'. With this one can say that preparation and standardization of tools is a major task as one has to take care in aspects like selection of area and sample, pooling up of statements related to the area, consulting the experts and application of sophisticated statistical techniques.

The second way of selection and use of tools is right selection of tools from already standardized ones available in the field of study. Here, also, it involves a tedious job in locating the tools and in identifying their usefulness to the study on hand. Even, then, this technique is very useful when the research work involves a good number of variables. Some people believe that some of the instruments available do not measure upto their standards. Hence new ones. In some instances, consideration is to be given to the logistics of the situation. Due to lacking of time and financial resources, many researchers may not produce a better instrument. In these cases, the most logical procedure that a researcher can follow is to choose the best instrument available for the purpose.

For the present study, the Self-Evaluation of Lessons checklist prepared in consultation with the available tools by Digumarti Bhaskara Rao was used to collect the data. "Self-Evaluation of lessons' (Appendix) was used by prospective teachers to express their opinion about their teaching. The prospective teacher has to attend the checklist after completing his or her teaching.

DATA COLLECTION

The 'Self-Evaluation of Lessons' checklist was given to the sampling unit after completing his/her lesson and asked to attend to the checklist, and finally got the self-evaluation of 96 prospective teachers. This data was used for statistical analysis to evaluate the teaching efficiency of prospective teachers.

4

ANALYSIS OF DATA

The next steps in the process of research after collection of data are the organization, analysis and interpretation of data and formulation of conclusions and generalizations to get a meaningful picture out of the raw information collected. The analysis and interpretation of data involve the objective material on the possession of the researcher and his subjective reactions and desires to derive from the data the inherent meanings in their relation to the problem (Rummel).

ANALYSIS OF DATA

Analysis of data usually means studying the material in order to determine inherent facts or meanings it involves breaking down the existing complex factors into simple parts and putting these parts together in new arrangements for purposes of interpretation.

The present chapter Analysis of Data, hence includes the analysis and interpretation of data and the results that resulted out of the analysis of data.

The Self Evaluation of lesson checklist consisted of Yes/No type response questions. The statistical treatment was given in the form of percentages to simplify the nature of the data. Thus, each statement in the tool gets a percentage for either Yes or No and by that its relative acceptance or usefulness can be known very easily.

As the tables are self-explanatory, much description of the components was not given. The readers can very easily grasp the results while going through the tables. The following are the results of the present study.

HYPOTHESIS 1

"The prospective teachers will have greater satisfaction about their teaching."

To test the above hypothesis the data was converted into percentages and the results are as follows.

Table 4.1 : Self-evaluation of lessons by prospective teachers (N=96)

S.No.	Component	Yes	%	No	%
1.	Did I achieve the objectives of my lesson ?	81	84.37	15	15.63
2.	Did I motivate effectively ?	86	89.58	10	10.42
3.	Did I stimulate the students to further learning ?	86	89.58	10	10.42
4.	Did I consider the individual differences ?	67	69.79	29	30.21
5.	Did I ask questions ?	92	95.83	04	04.17
6.	Did I rectify the students' faulty responses ?	84	87.50	12	12.50
7.	Did I utilize the students responses in developing the lession ?	84	87.50	12	12.50
8.	Did the students ask questions ?	33	34.38	63	65.62
9.	Did I use relevant audio visual aids ?	70	72.91	26	27.09
10.	Did I use audio visual aids successfully ?	63	65.62	33	34.38
11.	Did I use the chalk board to the full extent ?	85	88.53	11	11.47
12.	Did I draw clear diagrams on the chalk board ?	41	42.71	55	57.29
13.	Did I evaluate the major concepts as the lesson progressed ?	84	87.50	12	12.50
14.	Did I summarize the main concepts of the lesson ?	88	91.66	08	08.34
15.	Did I give home assignment ?	94	97.90	02	02.10
16.	Did I finish the lesson in time ?	90	93.74	06	06.26
17.	Did I follow the systematic procedure in presenting the lesson ?	90	93.74	06	06.26
18.	Did I supervise the class during teaching ?	86	89.58	10	10.42
19.	Did I maintain the discipline properly ?	80	83.33	16	16.67
20.	Did I experience any difficulty in the conduct of lesson ?	45	46.87	51	53.13
21.	Could I improve the lesson if I have second opportunity to teach the lesson ?	76	78.16	21	21.84

On the whole, the prospective teachers have greater satisfaction about their teaching. They have followed the techniques of teaching a lesson to the most possible extent, according to their personal opinion. Nearly three fourths of the teachers were of the opinion that they can improve their teaching if they get the second opportunity to teach the lesson.

The hypothesis that "the prospective teachers will have greater satisfaction about their teaching" can be accepted.

HYPOTHESIS 2

"There will be a significant difference in the teaching efficiency between the men and women prospective teachers."

To identify the difference between the teaching efficiency of men and women prospective teachers the following calculations were attended and the result are as follows.

Table 4.2 : Self-evaluation of lessons by men prospective teachers

(N=42)

S.No.	Component	Yes	%	No	%
1.	Did I achieve the objectives of my lesson ?	35	83.35	07	16.65
2.	Did I motivate effectively ?	39	92.87	03	07.13
3.	Did I stimulate the students to further learning ?	38	90.48	04	09.52
4.	Did I consider the individual differences ?	32	76.19	10	23.81
5.	Did I ask questions ?	40	95.26	02	04.74
6.	Did I rectify the students' faulty responses ?	38	90.48	04	09.52
7.	Did I utilize the students responses in developing the lession ?	34	80.97	08	19.03
8.	Did the students ask questions ?	21	50.00	21	50.00
9.	Did I use relevant audio visual aids ?	29	69.05	13	30.95
10.	Did I use audio visual aids successfully ?	24	57.15	18	42.85
11.	Did I use the chalk board to the full extent ?	33	78.57	09	21.43
12.	Did I draw clear diagrams on the chalk board ?	14	33.32	28	66.68
13.	Did I evaluate the major concepts as the lesson progressed ?	36	85.71	06	14.29
14.	Did I summarize the main concepts of the lesson ?	37	88.10	05	11.90
15.	Did I give home assignment ?	40	95.26	02	04.74
16.	Did I finish the lesson in time ?	39	92.87	03	07.13

(Contd.)

Table 4.2 : (Contd.)

S.No.	Component	Yes	%	No	%
17.	Did I follow the systematic procedure in presenting the lesson ?	37	88.10	05	11.90
18.	Did I supervise the class during teaching ?	37	88.10	05	11.90
19.	Did I maintain the discipline properly ?	35	83.35	07	16.65
20.	Did I experience any difficulty in the conduct of lesson ?	22	52.38	20	47.62
21.	Could I improve the lesson if I have second opportunity to teach the lesson ?	32	73.81	11	26.19

Table 4.3 : Self-evaluation of lessons by women prospective teachers (N=54)

S.No.	Component	Yes	%	No	%
1.	Did I achieve the objectives of my lesson ?	46	85.19	08	14.81
2.	Did I motivate effectively ?	47	87.04	07	12.96
3.	Did I stimulate the students to further learning ?	48	88.88	06	11.12
4.	Did I consider the individual differences ?	35	64.82	19	35.18
5.	Did I ask questions ?	52	96.30	02	03.70
6.	Did I rectify the students' faulty responses ?	46	85.19	08	14.81
7.	Did I utilize the students responses in developing the liession ?	50	92.06	04	07.40
8.	Did the students ask questions ?	12	22.24	42	77.76
9.	Did I use relevant audio visual aids ?	41	75.93	13	24.07
10.	Did I use audio visual aids successfully ?	41	75.93	13	24.07
11.	Did I use the chalk board to the full extent ?	52	96.30	02	03.70
12.	Did I draw clear diagrams on the chalk board ?	27	50.00	27	50.00
13.	Did I evaluate the major concepts as the lesson progressed ?	48	88.88	06	11.12
14.	Did I summarize the main concepts of the lesson ?	51	94.45	03	05.55
15.	Did I give home assignment ?	54	100.00	00	00.00
16.	Did I finish the lesson in time ?	51	94.45	03	05.55
17.	Did I follow the systematic procedure in presenting the lesson ?	53	98.15	01	01.85
18.	Did I supervise the class during teaching ?	49	90.74	05	09.26
19.	Did I maintain the discipline properly ?	45	83.33	09	16.67
20.	Did I experience any difficulty in the conduct of lesson ?	23	42.59	31	57.41
21.	Could I improve the lesson if I have second opportunity to teach the lesson ?	44	81.48	10	18.52

According to Table 4.2 and Table 4.3, both men and women prospective teachers have greater satisfaction towards their performance in their teaching. As per the tables, there was not much difference between these two categories in presenting the subject matter in their class rooms. Both of them have followed systematic procedure in their teaching. The men teachers failed in drawing the diagrams on the chalk board and they have also experienced a little difficulty in the conduct of their lessons when compared to their counter parts. Both the categories have felt that they can improve their teaching if they get an opportunity to teach again the same lesson, which shows their interest in improving the teaching efficiency of each lesson.

The hypothesis that "there will be a significant difference between the teaching efficiency of men and women prospective teachers" can be rejected.

HYPOTHESIS 3

"There will be a significant difference in the teaching efficiency between English and Telugu medium prospective teachers".

The following are the results related to hypothesis 3.

Table 4.4 : Self-evaluation of lessons by Telugu Medium prospective teachers

(N=74)

S.No	Component	Yes	%	No	%
1.	Did I achieve the objectives of my lesson ?	62	83.78	12	16.22
2.	Did I motivate effectively ?	64	86.50	10	13.50
3.	Did I stimulate the students to further learning ?	66	89.19	08	10.81
4.	Did I consider the individual differences ?	49	66.22	25	33.78
5.	Did I ask questions ?	71	95.94	03	04.06
6.	Did I rectify the students' faulty responses ?	63	85.12	11	14.88
7.	Did I utilize the students responses in developing the lession ?	65	87.84	09	12.16
8.	Did the students ask questions ?	26	35.14	48	64.86
9.	Did I use relevant audio visual aids ?	52	70.82	22	29.72
10.	Did I use audio visual aids successfully ?	48	64.86	26	35.14
11.	Did I use the chalk board to the full extent ?	67	90.55	07	09.45

(Contd.)

Table 4.4 : (contd.)

S.No.	Component	Yes	%	No	%
12.	Did I draw clear diagrams on the chalk board ?	32	43.24	42	56.76
13.	Did I evaluate the major concepts as the lesson progressed ?	62	83.78	12	16.22
14.	Did I summarize the main concepts of the lesson ?	68	91.83	06	08.17
15.	Did I give home assignment ?	73	98.65	01	01.35
16.	Did I finish the lesson in time ?	69	92.19	05	07.91
17.	Did I follow the systematic procedure in presenting the lesson ?	69	92.19	05	07.91
18.	Did I supervise the class during teaching ?	62	83.78	12	16.22
19.	Did I maintain the discipline properly ?	65	87.84	09	12.60
20.	Did I experience any difficulty in the conduct of lesson ?	31	41.90	43	58.10
21.	Could I improve the lesson if I have second opportunity to teach the lesson ?	54	72.95	20	27.05

Table 4.5 : Self-evaluation of lessons by English Medium prospective teachers

(N=22)

S.No.	Component	Yes	%	No	%
1.	Did I achieve the objectives of my lesson ?	19	86.38	03	13.62
2.	Did I motivate effectively ?	22	100.00	00	00.00
3.	Did I stimulate the students to further learning ?	20	90.90	02	09.10
4.	Did I consider the individual differences ?	17	77.27	05	22.73
5.	Did I ask questions ?	21	95.45	01	04.55
6.	Did I rectify the students' faulty responses ?	21	95.45	01	04.55
7.	Did I utilize the students responses in developing the lession ?	19	86.38	03	13.62
8.	Did the students ask questions ?	06	27.28	16	72.72
9.	Did I use relevant audio visual aids ?	19	86.38	03	13.62
10.	Did I use audio visual aids successfully ?	17	77.27	05	22.73
11.	Did I use the chalk board to the full extent ?	19	86.38	03	13.62
12.	Did I draw clear diagrams on the chalk board ?	10	45.45	12	54.55
13.	Did I evaluate the major concepts as the lesson progressed ?	21	95.45	01	04.55
14.	Did I summarize the main concepts of the lesson ?	21	95.45	01	04.55
15.	Did I give home assignment ?	21	95.45	01	04.55

(Contd.)

Table 4.5 : (contd.)

S.No.	Component	Yes	%	No	%
16.	Did I finish the lesson in time ?	20	90.90	02	09.10
17.	Did I follow the systematic procedure in presenting the lesson ?	21	95.45	01	04.55
18.	Did I supervise the class during teaching ?	21	95.45	01	04.55
19.	Did I maintain the discipline properly ?	20	90.90	02	09.10
20.	Did I experience any difficulty in the conduct of lesson ?	12	54.55	10	45.45
21.	Could I improve the lesson if I have second opportunity to teach the lesson ?	20	90.90	02	09.10

Out of the total sample nearly three fourths have taught in Telugu medium. Both the samples have felt that they have discharged the lesson to their best satisfaction. Both the samples have presented the subject matter in a systematic manner. They have failed only in drawing the diagrams on chalk board properly. English medium teachers have experienced some difficulty in the conduct of the lesson. Both the samples have felt that they can improve their teaching efficiency if they get another chance.

The hypothesis that "there will be a significant difference in the teaching efficiency between English and Telugu medium prospective teachers" can be rejected.

HYPOTHESIS 4

"There will be a significant difference in the teaching efficiency between the prospective teachers studying in aided and un-aided colleges of education."

Necessary statistical treatment was given to the data to test the above hypothesis and the results are as follows.

Table 4.6 : Self-evaluation of lessons by prospective teachers Studying in aided college of education

(N=52)

S.No.	Component	Yes	%	No	%
1.	Did I achieve the objectives of my lesson ?	43	82.70	09	17.30
2.	Did I motivate effectively ?	46	88.47	06	11.53
3.	Did I stimulate the students to further learning ?	47	90.38	05	09.62

(Contd.)

Table 4.6 : (Contd.)

S.No.	Component	Yes	%	No	%
4.	Did I consider the individual differences ?	34	65.38	18	34.62
5.	Did I ask questions ?	49	94.23	03	05.77
6.	Did I rectify the students' faulty responses ?	44	84.63	08	15.37
7.	Did I utilize the students responses in developing the lession ?	45	86.54	07	13.46
8.	Did the students ask questions ?	16	30.77	36	69.23
9.	Did I use relevant audio visual aids ?	34	65.38	18	34.62
10.	Did I use audio visual aids successfully ?	32	61.54	20	30.46
11.	Did I use the chalk board to the full extent ?	49	94.23	03	05.77
12.	Did I draw clear diagrams on the chalk board ?	30	57.69	22	42.31
13.	Did I evaluate the major concepts as the lesson progressed ?	47	90.38	05	09.62
14.	Did I summarize the main concepts of the lesson ?	50	96.16	02	03.84
15.	Did I give home assignment ?	50	96.16	02	03.84
16.	Did I finish the lesson in time ?	47	90.38	05	09.62
17.	Did I follow the systematic procedure in presenting the lesson ?	48	92.40	04	07.60
18.	Did I supervise the class during teaching ?	45	86.54	07	13.46
19.	Did I maintain the discipline properly ?	43	82.70	09	17.30
20.	Did I experience any difficulty in the conduct of lesson ?	24	46.15	28	53.85
21.	Could I improve the lesson if I have second opportunity to teach the lesson ?	37	71.15	15	28.85

Table 4.7 : Self-evaluation of lessons by prospective teachers studying in unaided college of education

(N=44)

S.No.	Component	Yes	%	No	%
1.	Did I achieve the objectives of my lesson ?	38	86.36	06	13.64
2.	Did I motivate effectively ?	40	90.90	04	09.10
3.	Did I stimulate the students to further learning ?	39	88.63	05	11.37
4.	Did I consider the individual differences ?	32	72.72	12	27.28
5.	Did I ask questions ?	43	97.72	01	02.28
6.	Did I rectify the students' faulty responses ?	40	90.90	04	09.10
7.	Did I utilize the students responses in developing the lession ?	39	88.63	05	11.37
8.	Did the students ask questions ?	15	34.09	29	65.91

(Contd.)

Table 4.7 : (Contd.)

S.No.	Component	Yes	%	No	%
9.	Did I use relevant audio visual aids ?	37	84.09	07	15.91
10.	Did I use audio visual aids successfully ?	33	75.00	11	25.00
11.	Did I use the chalk board to the full extent ?	36	81.81	08	18.19
12.	Did I draw clear diagrams on the chalk board ?	12	27.28	32	72.72
13.	Did I evaluate the major concepts as the lesson progressed ?	35	79.56	09	20.44
14.	Did I summarize the main concepts of the lesson ?	39	88.63	05	11.37
15.	Did I give home assignment ?	44	100.00	00	00.00
16.	Did I finish the lesson in time ?	44	100.00	00	00.00
17.	Did I follow the systematic procedure in presenting the lesson ?	42	95.43	02	04.57
18.	Did I supervise the class during teaching ?	41	93.17	03	06.83
19.	Did I maintain the discipline properly ?	38	86.36	06	13.64
20.	Did I experience any difficulty in the conduct of lesson ?	20	45.44	24	54.56
21.	Could I improve the lesson if I have second opportunity to teach the lesson ?	38	86.36	06	13.64

According to the Tables 4.6 and 4.7, there is not significant difference between the teaching efficiency of prospective teachers studying in aided and unaided colleges of education. Both the categories have taught well and they have greater satisfaction over their teaching. Both the samples have followed a systematic procedure in presenting the subject matter in the class. As usually, these also have felt that they can improve their teaching if they get second opportunity to teach the lesson.

The hypothesis that "there will be a significant difference between the teaching efficiency of prospective teachers studying in aided and un aided colleges of education' can be rejected.

5

SUMMARY, CONCLUSIONS AND DISCUSSION

Teaching is a social and professional activity. It is observable through teacher-behaviour or pupil-teacher interaction. It is measurable and quantifiable by observational techniques. It is a linguistic process. It is a prescription to the students. It involves encouraging, harmonizing, expressing and balancing functions. It is a high impact experience and a period of intense learning. However, the intense nature of the student learning experiences makes it a two-edged sword.

SUMMARY

Student teaching summary is a crucial phase of any teacher education programme. In India, we have a very good student teaching programme supervised by the teacher educators and teachers in the real class rooms. Even then, evaluation of teaching is very essential for its upgradation.

Considering the role of *self-evaluation of lessons* by the prospective teachers in enhancing their teaching efficiency, variables such as men versus women prospective teachers, English versus Telugu medium prospective teachers and aided versus un-aided college trained prospective teachers were selected.

Objectives were identified keeping the different aspects of the present study in view. The main objectives of the study were: 1. To identify the effectiveness of student teaching. 2. To identify the effectiveness of student teaching in terms of self-evaluation. 3. To identify the merits and limitations of student teaching. 4. To suggest appropriate measures to enhance the teaching effectiveness.

Hypotheses were formulated taking the above objectives into consideration. The main hypotheses of the present study were; 1. The prospective teachers will have greater satisfaction about their teaching, and 2. There will be a significant difference in the teaching efficiency of men and women, English and Telugu, and aided and unaided college prospective teachers.

In any research, various methods will be utilized for the selection of samples. After a detailed study of all these methods and considering the objectives and hypotheses selected for the study the *cluster sampling technique* was considered the best. Cluster sampling involves division of the population of elementary units under consideration into groups or clusters that serve as primary sampling units. The cluster sampling contains groups of elements instead of individual members or items in the population. For the present study two clusters were taken, namely. R.V.R. College of Education and A. L. College of Education. The prospective teachers were used as primary units.

Self Evaluation of Lessons checklist prepared by Digumarti Bhaskara Rao was used as tool for data collection from prospective teaches.

The raw data collected was put to statistical treatment. Only percentages of the opinions were considered so as to make the results so clear and easily understandable.

CONCLUSIONS AND DISCUSSION

The following are the findings of the study. Necessary discussion is followed the conclusions.

1. All the prospective teachers have expressed their satisfaction about their teaching. The objectives set for the lessons were achieved by eighty five percent of the sample. Nearly ninety percent of the sample felt that their motivation was effective.

Nearly ninety percent of the sample were of the opinion that their introduction stimulated the students to further learning. Seventy percent of the sample considered the individual differences in the class. Ninety percent of the teachers put questions in the class room to identify the understanding of the students. But, only fifty percent of the students asked the questions in the class. Eighty eight percent of the sample have rectified the faulty responses of the students and at the same time the same percentage of the sample have utilized the students' responses in developing their lesson. Seventy three percent of the sample have used the relevant audio visual aids, but only sixty six percent of the sample have felt that the use of such aids was successful. Eighty nine percent of the sample have used the chalk board to the full extent in writing, but only forty three percent of the sample have drawn the clear diagrams on the chalk board. Eighty eight percent of the sample have evaluated the major concepts of the lesson as the lessons progressed. Ninety two percent of the sample have summarized the lesson at its end. Except two percent of the teachers, others have given home assignment for further learning. Ninety four percent of the sample have finished the lessons within the given period of time. Except six percent, the remaining sample have followed systematic procedure in presenting the lesson. Ninety percent of the sample have supervised the class during teaching but only eighty three percent have managed proper discipline in the class. To a great surprise, forty seven percent of sample experienced difficulty in the conduct of the lesson though the lesson was presenting in the class at the end of the course training. But, it is happy to learn that seventy eight percent of prospective teachers have of the opinion that they can improve their teaching if they get a second opportunity to teach the lesson.

The result of the whole sample is of great interest to state that the sample has followed systematic procedure in presenting the lesson and has successfully completed it. As this is the opinion of the sample itself we can only say that the prospective teachers have great satisfaction over their teaching, which shows the effectiveness of the training provided in colleges of education. It is also a good sign to have a opinion of improving the lesson by additional teaching, which is a common phenomenon over the years of service. As they were teaching biology they must draw clear diagrams and they must also develop a questioning mind in the student community. The teachers must rectify the lapse that have come in their way of teaching.

2. Both men and women prospective teachers, on the whole, were with the opinion that they have completed their lessons effectively. Relatively the women teachers were a little bit more effective than their counter parts. Both the sub-samples have followed a systematic procedure in presenting the lessons. Fifty two percent of men teachers expressed difficulty in the conduct of the lesson while only forty three percent of women teachers have experienced difficulty in the conduct of lessons. Though the women teachers were relatively more effective they also wanted a second opportunity to teach the same lesson to improve their teaching efficiency.

   It is happy to learn that women are relatively a little bit more effective than their counter parts and this is an acceptable phenomenon as seen in many other observations and by many researches. On the whole, the difference between the two sub-samples is negligible and they can improve their teaching by developing interest, ability, creativity, etc., in teaching.

3. The prospective teachers teaching in Telugu and English media have great satisfaction over their teaching. English medium teachers have a negligible additional efficiency than their counter parts. Both the sub-samples have followed the systematic procedure in presenting the subject matter in the class.

   As the sub-samples have much satisfaction over their teaching they may not need much additional effort to improve their teaching efficiency. Still, as outsiders, we can suggest that they have to improve their teaching efficiency. The present study states that the language is not a barrier to teach effectively in any class.

4. The prospective teachers studying in aided and un-aided colleges of education have presented their lessons to their best satisfaction. Both the sub-samples have followed the systematic procedure in presenting the lessons. There is no significant difference in the teaching efficiency between these two sub-

samples.

In general, one may think that with great monitory benefits the teaching staff working in aided colleges of education may train more efficiently than their counterparts. The teacher educators working in the un-aided colleges of education may not work upto the expectations as they work with meager salaries, a general opinion. In contrast to this general opinion the prospective teachers of un-aided college of education have competed equally with the prospective teachers of aided college of education. The present study indicates that the monitory benefit of the teacher educators does not play any significant role in job satisfaction, but only the competition and the efficiency.

SUGGESTIONS FOR FURTHER RESEARCH

The present study brings light to the following areas for further research:

1. This study may be extended to a large sample taking some more variables.
2. This study may be extended to other disciplines and stages of teacher education.
3. Controlled and experimental groups may be considered in further studies.
4. Along with the self-evaluation, supervisor's evaluation may also be considered.
5. Evaluation may be taken up in micro-teaching also.
6. Suitable research tools may be developed by following proper procedures.
7. Studies may be taken up to develop uniform evaluation procedure through out the nation to get a standard teaching efficiency.
8. The recommendations of National Council of Teacher Education may be verified for their implementation in teacher education institutions.

BIBLIOGRAPHY

Aggarwal, Y.P.(1988). *Better Sampling: Concepts, Techniques; Evaluation*. New Delhi: Sterling Publishers.

Aggarwal, Y.P. (1974). *Survey of Audio Visual Materials at the Secondary Teacher Training Colleges*. New Delhi: NCERT.

AIATC(1964). *Symposium on Teachers Education in India*. Ambala Cantt : The Indian Publications.

Alpern, Moris L. (1946)). "The Ability to Test Hypothesis" *Science. Education* 30: 220-229.

Andrews, L.O. (1964). *Student Teaching*. New York: Centre for Applied Research in Education.

AITE (1970). *Curriculum Development in Teacher Education*. Bangkok: UNESCO.

AITE(1972). *Teacher Education in Asia—A Regional Survey*. Bangkok: UNESCO.

APEID (1975). *Alternative Structures and Methods in Teacher Education*. Bangkok: UNESCO.

APEID (1975). *Teacher Education and Curriculum Development*. Bangkok: UNESCO.

APEID (1976). *Exploring New Directions in Teacher Education*. Bangkok; UNESCO.

APEID (1977). *Exploring New Directions in Teacher Education: Orientating Teacher Education for Rural Devlopment*. Bangkok: UNESCO.

APEID (1977). *Reorienting Teacher Education for Rural Development*. Bangkok: UNESCO.

APEID (1979). *Teacher Education: Directions of Change*. Bangkok: UNESCO.

Banerjee, J.C. (1967). *Training of Primary School Teachers in India*. Doctoral Thesis, M.S. University of Baroda (Buch, ed.).

Bass, R.G. (1969). *Evaluation Procedures in Certain Primary Teacher Training Institutions in Asia*. Bangkok : UNESCO.

Benniw, W.A. (1961). "The Compensating Co operating Teachers" *Journal of Teacher Education*. 36: 131-133.

Best, John W. (1982). *Research in Education*. New Delhi: Prentice Hall of India.

Bhaskara Rao, D. (1986). "Effective Communication in Teaching". *Experiments in Education*. XIII: 109-111.

Bhaskara Rao, D. (1988). "An Evaluative Study of the Teaching Efficiency of Prospective Biological Science Teachers". *School Science*.

Bhaskara Rao, D. (1989). "Objectives of Sciene". *Science Promoter*.

Bhaskara Rao, D. (1989). *Dhrusyasravana Bodhanopakaranalu* (Audio Visual Teaching Aids). Guntur: Nagarjuna Publishers.

Bhaskara Rao, D. (1991). *Jeevasashtra Bodhana* (Teaching of Biology). Guntur: Nagarjuna Publishers.

Bhaskara Rao, D. (1993). *Vignanasashtra Bodhana* (Teaching of Science). Guntur: Creative Press.

Bhaskara Rao, D. (1994). *Scientific Aptitude*. New Delhi: Ashish Publishing House

Bhaskara Rao, D. (1995). *Animal Kingdom*. New Delhi: Discovery Publishing House.

Bhaskara Rao, D. (1995). *Batracalogy*. New Delhi: Discovery Publishing House.

Bhaskara Rao, D. (1995). *Vidyamanovignana Sashtram* (Educational Psychology). Guntur: Creative Press.

Bhaskara Rao, D. and D. Pushpa Latha (1995). *Achievement in Biology*. New Delhi: Discovery Publishing House.

Bhaskara Rao, D. and D. Pushpa Latha (1995). *Achievement in English*. New Delhi : Discovery Publishing House.

Bhaskara Rao, D. and D. Pushpa Latha (1995). *Achievement in Mathematics*. New Delhi Discovery Publishing House.

Bhaskara Rao, D. and D. Pushpa Latha (1995). *Achievement in Science*. New Delhi Discovery Publishing House.

Bhaskara Rao, D., C. Sridevi and K. Vijaya (1995). *Achievement in Social Studies*. New Delhi: Discovery Publishing House.

Bhaskara Rao, D. and K. Vijaya (1995). *A Text Book Evaluation*. Ambala Cantt: The Associated Publishers.

Bhaskara Rao, D. (1997). *Scientific Attitude*. New Delhi: Discovery Publishing House.

Bhaskara Rao, D. (1996). *Scientific Attitude vis-a-vis Scientific Aptitude*. New Delhi: Discovery Publishing House.

Bhaskara Rao, Digumarti, editor (1996). *Encyclopaedia of Education for all*. 5 Vols. New Delhi: APH Publishing Corporation.

Bhaskara Rao, Digumarti, editor (1996). *Global Perceptions on Peace Education*. 3 Vols. New Delhi : Discovery Publishing House.

Bhaskara Rao, Digumarti, editor (1996). *National Policty on Education*. 2 Vols. New Delhi: Anmol Publications.

Bhaskara Rao, Digumarti, editor (1997). *Reflections on Scientific Attitude*. New Delhi: Discovery Publishing House.

Bhaskara Rao, D. and L. Rathaiah, editors (1996). *International Innovations in Education*. New Delhi: Discovery Publishing House.

Bhaskara Rao, D. and K.R.S. Sambasiva Rao, editors (1996). *Current Trends in Indian Education*. New Delhi: Discovery Publishing House.

Bouri, H.H.A. (1965). "A Study into the Supervisors' Remarks" *Teacher Education* 9: 321-329.

Bouri, H.H.A. (1967). "Study, on Observed Lessons in Practice Teaching." *Indian Educational Review* 2: 131-134.

Bouri, H.H.A. (1970). "Search for Relationship between Theory and Practice Teaching." *Technical Teacher* 4 : 61-66.

Brown, J.D. (1979). *Teachers of Teachers*. London: Hodder and Stoughton.

Buch, M.B., editor (1974). *A Survey of Research in Education*. Baroda: CASE.

Buch, M.B., editor (1979). *Second Survey of Research in Education*. Baroda: SERD.

Buch, M.B., editor (1987). *Third Survey of Research in Education*. New Delhi: NCERT.

Buch, M.B. editor, *Fourth Survey of Research in Education*. New Delhi: NCERT.

Chatterjee, M.K. (1984). "Teacher Planning-cognitive Information Processing Approach". *Indian Educational Review*. 19:27-35.

Chourasia, G. (1967). *New Era in Teacher Education*. New Delhi: Sterling Publishers.

Cohen, I. and L. Manion (1977). *A Guide to Teaching Practice*. London: Methuen.

Copeland, W.D. (1981). "Clinical Experience in the Education of Teachers". *Journal of Education for Teaching*. 7:3-16.

Damodar, D. (1976). *A Critical Evaluation into the Practice of Student Teaching and Evaluation Programme in the Training Colleges of Andhra Pradesh*. Doctoral Thisis, M.S. University of Baroda (Bush, ed.).

Dave, R.H. and H.S. Srivastava (1968). "Methodology of Evaluating Educational Practices in Student Teaching." *Education and Psychology Review*. 8: 15-23.

Davis, M.D. (1976). "Eight Weeks versus Sixteen Weeks Student Teaching". *Journal of Educational Research*. 70:31-34.

Department of Teacher Education (1976). *Teacher Education: Problems and Perspectives—An Approach Paper*. New Delhi: NCERT.

Deshmukh, M.N. and C.K. Nagoshe (1981). "Evaluation of Practice Teaching: A Simple Tool". *Teacher Education*. 15: 139-147.

Dosajh, N.L. (1966). "Evaluation of Skills in Teaching". *Punjab Journal of Education*. 3: 74-79.

Dosajh, N.L. (1969)."A Study of Relationship between Qualifications of B.Ed. Trainees and Their Teaching Marks". *Indian Educational Review*. 4: 137-139.

Dossey, J.A. and L.H. Brown (1982). "Secondary School Mathematics Teacher Education at Illionois State University". *Journal of Educational Research and Development*. 15:75-77.

Ferguson, G. A. (1981). *Statistical Analysis in Psychology and Education*. Auckland: McGraw Hill.

Gage, N.L. (1966). *Handbook of Research on Teaching*. Chicago: Rand McNally.

Gage, N.L. (1978). *The Scientific Basis of the Art of Teaching*. New York: Teachers College, Columbia University.

Ganju, M.L. (1973). *A Study of the Preparation Programme of Graduate Teachers in Madhya Pradesh with a View to find out Changes Necessary for the Contemporary Madhya Pradesh*. Doctrol Thesis, Jabalpur University (Buch, ed.).

Griffiths, A.H. and A.H. Moore (1967)."Schools and Teaching Practice." *Education for Teaching*. 7: 33-39.

Gupta, S. (1977). *A Study of Some selected Inputs for Improving Education of Secondary School Teachers in Punjab-A Systems Approach*. Doctoral Thesis, M.S. University of Baroda (Buch, ed.).

Herbert, J. Walberg and G.D. Haertel (1990). *The International Encyclopaedia of Educational Evaluation*. Oxford: Pergamon Press.

Hoyle, E. (1970). "Planned Organisational Change in Education". *Research in Education*. 3:1–22.

John, J. and C.D. Foster (1976) *Teaching and Learning in the Elementary School*. New York: Macmillan Publishing Co.

Johnson, J.J. (1969). "Change in Student Teacher Dogmatism". *Journal of Educational Research*. 12: 224-226.

Joseph, K.J. (1967). *Teacher Education for Secondary Schools in Kerala*. Doctoral Thesis, University of Udaipur (Buch, ed.).

Joshi, D.C. (1967). "Supervision and Guidance—A Case Study of Three Student Teachers." *Teacher Education*. 1: 18-28.

Joshi, D.C. (1972). *A Study of Innovations and Changes in Teachers Colleges*. Doctoral Thesis, University of Udaipur (Buch, ed.).

Kawtra, P.S. (1980). "Teachers College Libraries in Orissa— A Study". *Journal of Indian Education*. 6:55-58.

Khan, M. (1983). *Teacher Education in India and Abroad*. New Delhi: Ashish Publishing House.

Khanpurkar, H.K. and U.K. Khanpurkar (1970). "An Experiment in Organising Student Teaching". *National Institute of Education Journal* . 5:5-10.

Kerlinger, F.N. (1964). *Foundations of Behavioural Research*. Holt, Rinehart and Winston.

Kohli, V.K. (1974). *A Critical Evaluation of Curriculum of Teacher Education of B.Ed. Level in Punjab*. Doctoral Thesis, M.S. University of Baroda (Buch, ed.).

Learning to Be. New Delhi: NCERT.

Marja, Talvi and D. Bhaskara Rao, editors (1996). *Educational Leadership and Social Changes*. New Delhi: Discovery Publishing House

Mallaya, V. (1968). *Teachers Training in Madhya Pradesh*. Doctoral Thesis, Sagar University (Buch, ed.).

Marker, N.S. (1976). *Survey of Teacher Education in the State of Maharashtra*. Doctoral thesis, University of Bombay (Buch, ed.).

Marlow Ediger and D. Bhaskara Rao (1996). *Science Curriculum*. New Delhi: Discovery Publishing House.

Mehrotra, R.N. (1973). "Effects of Teacher Education Programmes on the Attitude of Teachers Towards Teaching Profession". *Teacher Education*. 8: 27-39.

Mehrotra, S.N. (1972). "Planning Training Programmes for Science and Mathematics Teachers". *Teacher Today*. 14:9-18.

Mohanty, S.B. (1987). *Student Teaching*. New Delhi: Ashish Publishing House.

Morris, S. and E. Stines (1972). "The Assessment of Practical Teaching". *Educational Research*. 14:110-119.

Mukherji, S.N., editor (1968). *Education of Teachers in India*. Delhi: S. Chand & Co.

Naidu, R. V. (1975). "Student Teachers' Attitude Towards Internship of Teaching". *Teacher Education*. 9:44-47.

NCERT (1969). *Second Survey of Teacher Education in India*.

NCERT (1978). *Teacher Education Curriculum*: A Framework.

Palsane, M.N. and D.A. (1957). "Practice Teaching". *Teacher Education*. 1:1-37.

Pondey, B.N. and D.N. Khosla (1974). *Student Teaching and Evaluation : A Handbook for Secondary Colleges of Education*. New Delhi: NCERT.

Pangotra, N.N. (1979). "Final Teaching Marks of B.Ed. Students and their Subsequent success as Teachers". *Journal of Educational research and Extension*. 16 : 59-63.

Pant, S.C. (1975). "Mechanics of Internship". *Teacher Education*. 9:37-43.

Patel, R.N. (1979). "An Analysis of Performance of B.Ed. Students with respect to their Practice Teaching". *Journal of Educational Research and Extension*. 16 : 15-17.

Piers, E.A. (1967). *Student Teaching Practices in Primary Teacher Training Institutions in Asia*. Bangkok: UNESCO.

Price, R.D. (1961). "The Influence of Supervising Teachers". *Journal of Teacher Education*. 12:471–475.

Rai, V.K. (1983)."Problems of Student Teaching—An Opinion Survey". *Experiments in Education*. 11:134-137.

Rathaiah, L. and D. Bhaskara Rao (1996). *Achievement Correlates.* Ambala Cantt: The Indian Publishers.

Rastogi, K.G. (1969). *Supervision of Practice Teaching*. New Delhi: CIE.

Rummel, J. Francis (1958). *An Introduction to Research Procedures in Education*. New York: Harper and Brothers.

Sadasivan Nair, V. and K. Kulandaivel (1977). "Evaluation of the B.T. Programme by Trained Graduate Teachers". *Journal of Educational Research and Extension*. 8:188-190.

Sanjeeva Rao, P.C. (author) and D. Bhaskara Rao (editor) Applied Science Series (1996). *A Text Book of Geology*. New Delhi. Discovery Publishing House.

Shah, B.A. (1974). *A Comparative Study of the Teacher Education Programmes for Secondary Teachers in U.K. and U.S.A. with Special Reference to India*. Doctoral thesis, Sardar Patel University (Buch, ed).

Shankar, U. (1984). *Education of Indian Teacher*. New Delhi: Sterling Publishers.

Sharma, S. (1970). "Relation of Achievement in Theory and Practice Teaching in B.Ed. Examination". *Quest in Education*. 7:41-45.

Sharma, S.L. (1973). *Evaluation of Practice Teaching Programme of Post-Graduate Teacher Training Programmes in U.P.* Doctoral thesis, Aligarh Muslim University (Buch, ed.).

Sharma, T.R. and A. Kaur (1970). "Training in the Teaching of Punjabi in the Post-Graduate Teacher Training Programmes in the Punjab". *Indian Educational Review*. 5:19-29.

Shukla, R.S. (1976). *An Investigation into the Secondary Teacher Education Programme in Orissa—A Critical and Constructive Study*. Doctoral thesis, Utkal University (Buch, ed.).

Singh, L. P. (1980). "Lifelong Education and Teacher Preparation". *Teacher Today*. 22:46-48.

Singh, V. and S.M. Nayer (1970). "A Study of the Problems of Pupil Teachers in Practice Teaching Area of Teacher Education Programme". *Teacher Education*. 4 : 32-37.

Smith, S.D. and W.D. Smith (1979). "Teaching the Poor: Its Effect on Student Teaching". *Journal of Teacher Education*. 30:45-49.

Srinivasacharyulu, G. (1979). "An Investigaion into the Attitude of Teacher Trainees Towards Practical Aspects of B.Ed. Programmes". *Experiments in Education*. 7:145-148.

Srivastava, R.C. (1970). *Evaluation of Practice Teaching in Teacher Training Institutions.* Delhi: CIE.

Tudhope, W.B. (1942). "A Study of the Training College Final mark as Criterion of future Success in the Teaching Profession". *British Journal of Educational Psychology*. 12:167-171.

UNESCO (1979). *Directory of Innovative Institutions Preparing Educational Personnel.* Paris: UNESCO.

Veena Kumari, B. and D. Bhaskara Rao (1996). *Operation Blackboard.* New Delhi: Ashish Publishing House.

Venkata Rao, P, and D. Bhaskara Rao (1989). *A Textbook Zoology—Junior Intermediate.* Guntur : Vignan Publishers.

Venkata Rao, P. and D. Bhaskara Rao (1989). *A Textbook of Zoology-Senior Intermediate.* Guntur: Vignan Publishers.

Vidya, C. (author) and D. Bhaskara Rao (editor, Applied Science Series) (1996). *A Text Book of Nutrition.* New Delhi: Discovery Publishing House.

Wilkinson, R.D. (1963). "Evaluation based upon Observation Reports of Supervisors of Student Teachers". *Journal of Educational Research*. 56: 264-271.

Williams, C.M., R.M. Deever and E.B. Jr. Flynn (1960). "Professional Laboratory Experiences in Oklahama". *Journal of Teacher Education*. 11: 497-505.

Wiseman, S. and K.B. Start (1964). "A Follow-up of Teachers Five Years after Completing their Training". *British Journal of*

Educational Psychology. 29: 342-361.

Warren Little, Judith (1993). "Teachers' Professional Development and Educational Reform". *CPRE Policy Briefs.*

APPENDIX

SELF-EVALUATION OF LESSONS

Dear Student Teacher,

Self-evaluation of lessons plays a major role in improving the teaching capacity and to rectify the errors committed in the previous classes. To do this job, a check-list is given to you to evaluate your lesson by yourself. This check-list is to be used to arrive at conclusions and to suggest positive measures. You are hereby requested to go through the tool and put a tick (✓) mark against the choice based on your opinion immediately after the completion of your lesson. Your cooperation is highly solicited.

Thanking you,

Friendly Yours,

(Investigator)

Name:	Qualifications:	Sex :	Age:
Lesson:		Class:	

1.	Did I achieve the objectives of my lesson ?	Yes	No
2.	Did I motivate effectively ?	Yes	No
3.	Did I stimulate the students to further learning ?	Yes	No
4.	Did I consider the individual differences ?	Yes	No
5.	Did I ask questions ?	Yes	No
6.	Did I rectify the students' faulty responses ?	Yes	No
7.	Did I utilize the students' responses in developing the lession ?	Yes	No
8.	Did the students ask questions ?	Yes	No
9.	Did I use relevant audio visual aids ?	Yes	No
10.	Did I use audio visual aids successfully ?	Yes	No
11.	Did I use the chalk board to the full extent ?	Yes	No
12.	Did I draw clear diagrams on the chalk board ?	Yes	No
13.	Did I evaluate the major concepts as the lesson progressed ?	Yes	No
14.	Did I summarize the main concepts of the lesson ?	Yes	No
15.	Did I give home assignment ?	Yes	No
16.	Did I finish the lesson in time ?	Yes	No
17.	Did I follow the systematic procedure in presenting the lesson ?	Yes	No
18.	Did I supervise the class during teaching ?	Yes	No
19.	Did I maintain the discipline properly ?	Yes	No
20.	Did I experience any difficulty in the conduct of lesson ?	Yes	No
21.	Could I improve the lesson if I have second opportunity to teach the lesson ?	Yes	No

INDEX